IRRITABLE BOWEL SYNDROME

A Self-Help Guide

John Elsdon

*First published in Great Britain in 1993 by Carnell Limited,
37 Salisbury House, London Wall, London EC2M 5PJ.*

Copyright © 1993 by Carnell Limited.

Typeset by SJ Design and Publishing, Bromley, Kent.

Printed by Repro City Limited, London.

ISBN 1-85779-133-9

Foreword
by
Dr Andrew Llewelyn

Irritable Bowel Syndrome

The Irritable Bowel Syndrome is the most common gastro-intestinal disease seen by doctors in general clinical practice. Although it is not a life-threatening illness, it causes great distress to those it afflicts and often brings a feeling of helplessness and frustration to the physician attempting to treat it.

This John Elsdon book clearly outlines the most frequently found manifestations of the Irritable Bowel Syndrome and clarifies them with some excellent case summary descriptions. The variety of the symptoms that can result from the Irritable Bowel Syndrome is described in a clear and non-clinical way, so that self-diagnosis and self-learning of this very difficult condition become a realistic possibility.

Later in the book, the suggestions on the management of this condition are made in a practical way, so that those affected by the Irritable Bowel Syndrome and its attendant conditions will be able to find some useful tips on how to minimise their symptoms and reduce the impact of the Irritable Bowel Syndrome on their lives.

To a doctor, the diagnosis of the Irritable Bowel Syndrome is suggested primarily by the long duration of symptoms without obvious signs of physical deterioration, together with the intermittent character of the disability and the relation of symptoms to environmental or emotional stress. To the physician, each case presenting itself with what may even occasionally seem like minor symptoms, deserves careful consideration and may require extensive investigation at some point.

With the information available in this book, any person suffering from Irritable Bowel Syndrome will clearly be able to identify themselves and make the most of the self-help plans included.

Additionally, with dietary advice and the use of some pharmaceutical preparations which are now available, symptomatic relief from this condition can often be obtained. For those suffering from this chronic and debilitating condition, this book clearly offers a light at the end of the tunnel.

Andrew Llewelyn MB BS BSc

This book is not intended to be a
substitute for medical advice or
treatment. Self-diagnosis can be
dangerous. If you have any health
problem, see your doctor promptly.

Table of Contents

1 Meet The Enemy

Irritable Bowel Syndrome is the name given to a medical condition which we have all probably experienced at some time. It mostly shows itself as constipation, diarrhoea, rumbling tummy, stomach pain, heartburn and flatulence. Sometimes these manifestations of Irritable Bowel Syndrome (IBS) are all present in the same six hour period, whilst at other times a sufferer can go from a bout of constipation to serious diarrhoea within an hour, or even in the space of a month.

This variety of symptoms and effects straightaway shows us the complexity of IBS. It explains why:

(a) it is necessary to write a book about it;

(b) there is no known single cause;

(c) doctors cannot agree a single effective cure;

(d) quite often the only advice is to 'live with it'.

Happily, the 'living with it' dismissal means that the complaint is not considered to be serious enough for intensive medical attention, but its inconveniences can be considerably eased and the effects even totally cleared by a combination of medical advice and self-help.

KNOWLEDGE IS POWER

If you suspect that you have Irritable Bowel Syndrome, you will be better able to explain the feelings and effects of the complaint to your doctor and you will more properly understand the remedies he proposes, if you have some knowledge of yourself and how your bodily functions work.

That is another reason for publishing this new handbook and why we are sure that you can get some comfort, confidence, calm and easement from reading it. It is a work of optimism which hopes to help any sufferer to help themselves back to perfect health.

Right from the outset, it must be emphasised that these pages are in no way a substitute for professional medical help. A doctor will always be the first line of consultation and the most sure line of cure. There is absolutely no other course of action than to make an appointment with your doctor if you feel that you are a long-term IBS sufferer, or that bouts of the symptoms which we shall later describe in detail are becoming frequent, or more severe.

However, you will be much more enthusiastic about taking prescribed medicine or doing the physio's exercises if you understand just how and why these things are doing you good.

A doctor is only as good as the information which the patient gives him. Some medical conditions obviously have very visible symptoms, but many can only be diagnosed from the information which the sufferer can give the doctor. So, without becoming a hypochondriac, the more we know about ourselves, the more we are likely to be able to help the doctor to cure us. IBS is such a wide and sometimes imprecise series of maladies that a greater shared understanding between sufferer and healer can only do good.

YOU ARE NOT ON YOUR OWN

The inspiration for doing the research for and preparing this self-help guide comes as a result of being a sufferer. In this suffering, I am not alone. It is estimated that about 15 per cent of both the child and the adult population are chronic sufferers of IBS and that a further 25 per cent are subject to periodic and protracted bouts of the complaint. In fact, we are all attacked by IBS in some form or other at some maybe very brief – moments in our lives.

"I had a knot in the gut about that" is just one of the commonplace phrases uttered at times of panic that illustrate the connection between stress and the side-effects from needing to rush to the loo, or getting

a rumbling tummy or even a pain in the stomach. We shall discuss this in more detail in chapter seven.

The complexity of IBS, and why so many people are uncomplaining sufferers, is further illustrated by a whole vocabulary of phrases which we all use and which relate to the human being's eating, digestive and defecation processes. They underline the importance of our insides and why any malfunction of the stomach can upset the sufferer's emotions and vice versa.

"He didn't have the stomach for the job."
"He had no guts."
"She was belly-aching all evening."
"I had real butterflies in my stomach."
"I had this feeling in the pit of my stomach."
"He's a real pain in the backside."
"She'd had a real bellyful of it all."
"He's got fire in his belly."

These expressions have evolved over many centuries, but they still serve to illustrate the importance of our bowels and bodily functions and how they can be influenced by so many seemingly unconnected factors. It partly shows how IBS really is universal. There is much more of it about than most of us think. There is much more about than is ever brought to the doctor's attention. This is to be regretted, because IBS might well be the root-cause of many other irritants from head-ache and depression to belching and aching joints. The advice bears repeating. If you recognise the symptoms, consult your doctor.

The biggest problem is that many IBS sufferers do not believe that they have a medical malfunction. They see the syndrome as an inconvenience without cure and probably brought on by something they ate, a heavy night, or just bolting lunch in order to keep an appointment. They kid themselves that it will all sort itself out tomorrow, or that it will all go away come the relaxation of the weekend.

But it doesn't! So they further delude themselves with the excuse that the break was just not long enough, but it will be okay when next weekend comes, or in two months when they are due to take a holiday.

Thus, they go on suffering and spoiling their lives – and possibly those of family and friends – because any expedition which is far from a toilet cannot be undertaken. There are youngsters who will not take a girlfriend out to dinner, simply because they know that they will get flatulent. Rumbling tummy in the romantic bed is just as bad.

IBS sufferers generally suffer in silence. That is a big mistake. You should always talk to somebody – especially a doctor.

We have all met people who love to talk about their imperfect medical history and there are some illnesses which are acceptable as dinner-table talk – even for boasting over coffee and brandy. When I worked as a lecturer, it seemed that almost every other student in my tutorial group was having a 'nervous breakdown'. It was so common-place that it was mostly referred to just by its initials. If you were not close to a NB, you were not working hard enough. Similarly, migraine, hardened arteries, cataract and heart problems are all 'clean' com-plaints suitable for public confession and airing.

On the other hand, Irritable Bowel Syndrome sounds as though it is 'not quite nice'. Irritable connotes scratching or itching, and there is something very nasty about your bowel, gut, intestines, urine and faeces. Understandably, they have become a taboo topic of conversation in genteel Western society. You can tell your hostess that you do not eat heavily-salted items because they increase your blood pressure, but you can scarcely refuse with the excuse that *"It will probably make me flatulent"*.

In fact, IBS is such a 'tacky' topic that many sufferers cannot even find the words to describe the symptoms to the doctor, or they feel too embarrassed to talk it over with him. So they suffer in silence and this is plain daft, because it will not go away without some help. You must also remember that you will not embarrass your doctor by precise descriptions of unpleasant things. He is dealing with matters even worse than IBS every day of his life. He will want to help you.

The other problem is indecision. If you break a leg, you know that you have done it, can locate the trauma very precisely and can tell the doctor where it hurts. It is a very recognisable problem in the same way that toothache, a boil, bruising, headache and joint pains are easily pinpointed and described.

On the other hand, IBS covers such a wide spectrum of aches, pains and inconveniences affecting parts of the body which you cannot see and which are so badly understood by most of us that we back off even trying to tell anybody about them. The whole thing seems too vague even though its effects are very evident.

We shall discuss the interaction of worry causing IBS and vice versa later on. Here we should just mention that a good number of people fear going to the doctor over a seemingly minor internal complaint just in case he diagnoses something more serious. Cancer, 'The Big C', is one real fear.

Here I cannot appeal too strongly that you overcome the fear. The more you worry about a more serious illness the more irritated your bowel is likely to become and the more your day-to-day life will be ruined.

Worry is a pointless emotion. Easy to say, but also brought into perspective by an anecdote in Winston Churchill's history of Hitler's War. He recalled a man who confessed in his last moments that much of his life had been ruined by problems and difficulties which never actually happened.

Irritable Bowel Syndrome is not a disease for which surgery or other unpleasant remedies must be undergone. It does not automatically lead to serious complications and will not degenerate into cancer or Crohn's disease. Nobody has ever died as a direct result of IBS.

The cause might be one of many and there are several methods of relief and sometimes total cure. If complete healing is not achieved, there are a number of ways of lessening the effects and of making IBS easier to live with. The complaint itself is also very responsive to the sort of self-help which the following pages contain.

There is always comfort in numbers. IBS affects millions of ordinary people, who go on living their lives more or less normally, but who would be much happier if the irritants could be eased or extinguished.

It is also significant that any radio/television programme or magazine article discussing IBS generates a vast correspondence and it was far ahead of any other topic when the publishers asked newspaper readers which medical complaints caused them most concern. You are not alone in your doubts.

A problem shared is a problem halved. So share the problem with your doctor and see this book as a way of getting a common language and a basis for mutual understanding. Even if it just fills in some of the gaps between you and your doctor, it will still have earned its place on your bookshelf.

2 An Irritable Bowel Study

The study of the Irritable Bowel Syndrome is one of fascination and frustration. It is not a classic complaint for which a medical team can offer a classic cure. IBS has no single known cause and no panacea. There is no known magic wand which can be waved either to diagnose the condition with certainty, or to prescribe an assured remedy.

Absolutely everybody will develop some of the annoying, inconvenient symptoms at some time in their life. You are probably reading this book because you feel that you are a fellow sufferer, either very briefly at times of real panic, or in the short-term when *"things just aren't going well at the moment"*, or you have the manifestations over a longer period and *"feel out of sorts"*, disgusted with yourself. Some sufferers even feel a little bit dirty.

Doctors have two distinct attitudes and totally different approaches when confronted with the hotch-potch of moans, groans and effects which IBS commonly causes. These symptoms or irritants themselves also help to worsen the condition.

Some doctors use the phrase Irritable Bowel Syndrome as an umbrella name for a set of inconveniences which will disappear with time, or when you can be persuaded to lose a stone in weight, take a bit of exercise, lay off the drink or go somewhere warm for a holiday.

The second group of medics recognise that there must be a root-cause – even several root-causes – for everything, so they are not dismissive and are willing to spend time and effort in detailed diagnosis.

Strangely enough, both types of doctor can be correct in their attitudes and treatment. As the group of case histories which follows will illustrate, the Irritable Bowel Syndrome is like a pendulum swinging between the physical and the psychological. If you ride the pendulum, the more IBS symptoms you acquire, the more you worry about them, so this anxiety makes the diarrhoea, constipation, full feeling and flatulence get worse.

This means that the doctor who tells you to relax is right. The doctor who shows you how to relax is even better. Equally, the medical adviser who seeks a purely physical cause and cure can also be correct and will diminish your tension as his treatment succeeds.

If you feel that IBS is a chicken and egg situation, you are correct, but you will have the comfort of knowing that there are millions like you and that every day hundreds of thousands of them are given relief by doctors, or they help themselves to improve their condition. Between your doctor, yourself and the understanding which we are trying to bring, the syndrome might well disappear altogether, just like it has for some of the sufferers profiled below.

Medical records contain millions of IBS cases and they are all roughly the same in some ways, yet they are all also different in others. If you are a sufferer, you will probably be similar to most, but not be completely the same as anybody else. For that reason – and because of doctor/patient confidentiality – we have given the stories of four people, using fictitious names, passed on to us by medical friends. You could see yourself in any of them, or in all of them.

Study One – Don – Age 42

BACKGROUND

Don is a police sergeant. One might say that he is a reluctant policeman who joined the force because that is what his family always did. He has never been enthusiastic about the job and feels stuck because several times he has been passed over for promotion. He hates going in to work, is frequently off sick with minor ailments and is ticking off the days, months and years until retirement and pension.

IBS HISTORY

The diarrhoea, bowel rumblings and constantly feeling bloated started about six years ago. The nearest, recognisable, possibly significant, important personal event was a period of hospitalisation following semi-serious injuries received whilst policing a fracas outside a disco. Because of complications, Don was treated by massive doses of antibiotics and other curative chemicals. When the IBS symptoms began to develop and to accelerate, his own 'gut feeling' was that his system had been upset by the injuries and the curing agents.

Don went through a two-year period of bubbling, noisy belly and occasional sharp stomach stabs. Very often, he felt a sudden, desperate urge to use the toilet, but when he got there could not make a bowel action. At other times, the defecation was so massive and so prolonged that he felt that he had not only emptied his intestines but had also passed out part of their internal structure. There were also short bouts of a slightly burning lower stomach pain.

Don applied for early retirement, but this was turned down because of insufficient medical grounds. The specialist told him that the problem would vanish with time, especially if Don stopped worrying, took on more fresh fruit and much less alcohol. Our subject felt this was a sop to get him out of the surgery.

He also realised that the application for early retirement was a professional, tactical error which would totally destroy his chances of promotion. His salary and prospects were now irrevocably pegged at their present level. That was at once worrying and debilitating. The IBS symptoms just got worse.

Don is not stupid. He observed that the flatulence and diarrhoea became worse when: (1) he took strenuous exercise or was forced into physical exertion; (2) after dinner parties; (3) if he worried about work. He further noticed that the inconvenience attacks and the short-lived stabbing pains were becoming more frequent. He had also read too many medical books which he did not fully understand and began to worry that he might have stomach cancer, ulcerative colitis or Crohn's disease.

Don was so worried that he paid for a private comprehensive internal and external medical examination. This confirmed that he was not suffering from any abdominal and rectal disease or injury. There was nothing demonstrably wrong, so he should just stop worrying. This is much easier to say than to do.

Police work gives you plenty of contacts and Don's best was a friendly GP – not his own. This doctor listened well and asked lots of questions about lifestyle, eating habits, the job and medication. Then he thought about it for a week before calling Don back and telling him that he was suffering from Irritable Bowel Syndrome.

The doctor suggested a programme of self-help, comprising:

(1) A change of two items of diet for a fortnight, ie cut out coffee and potatoes. If Don felt that there was any improvement, he should reintroduce one of them and observe the effects.

(2) Get a book on relaxation and take thirty minutes of each meal break to do some of the things it suggests.

(3) Take moderate but regular exercise such as a fast walk or a session on the police rowing machine, plus deep breathing exercises every morning.

The doctor friend oozed confidence and enthused *"I am sure that we've cracked it. You will soon start to get better."*

Don did and has continued to lose, or greatly to diminish, all the symptoms and irritants of last year.

Study Two – Anna – Age 28

BACKGROUND

Anna is a very good looking girl who works as a dealer for a finance and stockbroking agency. She is a high-flyer destined for one of the best jobs in her profession and the top of the social tree. She lives with her boyfriend, who has a similar well-paid job and lifestyle.

IBS HISTORY

Anna noticed that she was increasingly getting acid stomach with bouts of near vomiting when an acidic liquid came up as far as her mouth and was re-swallowed. She was also needing to urinate quite frequently and experiencing spasmodic tightening of the stomach area.

These circumstances coincided with (or came just after) her accidental sighting of her own, in-house, confidential record file. She learned that she was one of two dealers in the running for Section Head and a huge salary increase. The promotion would depend on performance – ie, how much profit she made for the company – and on how well she was observed to get on with her colleagues.

With hindsight, Anna wishes that she had never seen that file but, excited, she launched herself into a frenzy of work and a carousel of parties, discos and dinners with workmates. The hours were irregular and the tension enjoyably high, so Anna did not really notice the creeping symptoms of increasing flatulence and the alternating bouts of constipation and loose bowel. The stomach pains she put down to the menstrual cycle.

Neither (at the time) did she notice her inability to relax – to read, to watch television or to sit at home for a quiet evening with Jack. She felt that she was in a passing phase of being hyperactive, excited, on a bit of a high and enjoying it.

Inevitably, Anna pulled a couple of bum deals which lost money, so she worked even more hours to regain the finance. On occasions, Jack was not at home when she returned and when she got home early she was too tired for cooking, or any other pleasure.

Jack went back to squash and golf and one night did not come home at all. The promotion did not seem to be in too much of a hurry to show and Anna began to have doubts about herself. She was worried that Jack might move out and leave her with massive mortgage and car repayment bills. She was now also anxious about her very frequent 'peptic tummy'. Did she have the beginnings of a serious illness?

Things came to a head with such a serious bout of gastric flu that Anna was taken into her private medical subscription clinic. After this, nothing seemed to get better. The acidity increased as did the number of sudden urges to go to the loo, where her bowels initially behaved normally and without pain.

She started to resist these calls of nature and this caused headaches. Anna felt very bloated even half way through normal meals. The following morning she was always very 'windy' with belching and flatulence which got to embarrassing levels during menstruation. At these times, the headaches were very fierce and often followed by three or four days of total constipation.

"The most embarrassing part was the flatulence and tummy rumbling in our confined work space. I might have been wrong, but I felt that the other dealers were making jokes about me."

The doctor who had treated the gastric flu acknowledged those symptoms that Anna was willing to talk about and confided that *"It is just a phase that all you young women go through."*

Our subject was driven to trying all the home remedies – Milk of Magnesia, Alka Seltzer, a diet of chicken and fish, she cycled to work and went close to being teetotal. Anna was almost paranoid about her incurable condition. None of this appeased Jack, who wanted to separate.

Finally, Anna leaned on the company's insurances and consulted a medical psychologist. For the visit, she took a long, written list of everything she felt to be important or contributing – both physical and mental. The lady doctor spent two hours with Anna and made a second appointment which would be shared with a physician colleague specialising in gastro and abdominal disorders.

The team of doctors told her that she was suffering a series of minor stresses and strains collecting themselves together as Irritable Bowel Syndrome. Their suggested cure was to defuse the panic about promotion by discreetly contacting other brokers to see if they might have any openings. This done and proven positive Anna took the advice not to ask her boss, but to tell him, that she was exhausted and was taking a month's holiday – paid or unpaid she did not care.

The holiday was to be in the sun with nothing to do but swim, laze and read fiction and should encompass a total change of diet by going on to local foods and wines. The doctors advised eating what she enjoyed and to lap up all the attention such a pretty girl would surely get.

The case is now closed. Anna's bowel problems diminished during the holiday. In her absence she was headhunted by a rival broker and now has a well-paid job with a contract which limits her hours of work. She has a new boyfriend and has taken up painting and the new companion's boat.

The symptoms of IBS diminished in six months and totally disappeared after a year. Anna's periods are normal and the headaches rare. True, there is a regression if she overeats or gets hung over, but as long as she perseveres with her interesting new normality, Anna can go out in confidence and works enough to do her job well without trying to do it too well.

Study Three – Alec – Age 45

BACKGROUND

Alec was made redundant by a communications company, so used his pay-off, plus some grants, to set up a one-man business installing office and shop telephone and intercom systems. This occurred in boom time for the enterprise culture of easy bank loans and all forecasts promised a good income for Alec, his wife, plus two sons, plus dog, plus mortgage, plus car on HP and a mini for the family runabout.

Within a year, Alec had saturated the local area and was needing to travel much further afield to find new customers. The selling part of his business became much harder and the installations more costly to service. There was a genuine worry that the cash flow would dry up.

At this same time, the bank began to get fidgety about the overdraft and were demanding settlement, or hinting that they would need his house remortgaged as their collateral. Alec's wife was now also needed in the business, so she gave up her nursing job.

IBS HISTORY

Alec subsequently recalls, *"At about this time I was always tired and mostly worried about money and the future. I was very tense and used to swing between bouts of gluttony for junk food and cheap wine to periods where I would storm out to go walking on the Moors and eat nothing all day. This gave me a funny taste in my mouth, diarrhoea and all sorts of stomach pains, which never seemed to be in the same place."*

Eventually, Alec went to see his doctor, who performed a very thorough examination and diagnosed spastic colon. He explained that the muscles which move the food along the intestines were out of synchronisation and squeezing when they should have been relaxed. He prescribed some pills called anti-spasmodics to help the muscles relax. He advised increasing the roughage and fibre in each meal and laying off the booze. He also strongly advised losing at least a stone in weight.

This all made sense to Alec so he complied but, alas, it did not work. If anything, the irritants got worse. Most worrying was the periodic sharp pain, which led the sufferer to worry that he might have cancer, so he changed to another doctor.

"This new chap looked at my notes and told me much the same and that I should just be patient. He flatly refused any NHS tests and was a bit blunt. He was quite rude when he said that there were thousands like me who just had to live with the upset stomach which would go if I was patient and followed advice."

By this time Alec was desperate enough for anything, so he went to see an osteopath, whose signboard also listed a number of other skills from acupuncture to dietetics. He told Alec that he believed in 'total medicine', meaning that every part and function of the body is inter-connected *"from brain to bowel"*. If it was all out of kilter, the only remedy would be a total change of lifestyle.

"I took this along to my second new NHS doctor and she did a full set of tests before telling me that I had Irritable Bowel Syndrome and that the lay medico's suggested cure made a lot of sense."

During the same period, the telephone business was obviously collapsing, so Alec sold off enough to pay the bank without putting his house at risk and took a job as a minibus driver. He enjoyed this and was made an inspector within a year and became the City's Assistant Transport Manager a year later.

Alec is now a very contented man whose stomach pains are virtually non-existent. There are no rumbling noises down below and he enjoys digestion without complaint.

Study Four – Lisa – Age 22

BACKGROUND

Lisa is a university student of philosophy. In character she is very outward going, very proud, very competitive and has represented her college at squash, hockey and tennis. She admits to being a study and fitness fanatic.

IBS HISTORY

In her second year, Lisa began to experience periodic stomach pains, usually followed by mild diarrhoea and the need to go to the toilet about ten times a day, often at very short notice.

The college doctor diagnosed IBS, but could not suggest any sure cure other than to get her to do less and not to worry about her academic and sporting performance. Relax! Enjoy yourself! 'Think what a lucky girl I am', seemed to be the message.

Unfortunately, this proved to be too difficult and the bowel complaints not only became worse, but were also joined by a feeling of sickness. These parts of the syndrome themselves became worse before exams and big matches. Three months after her visit to the doctor, Lisa underwent bouts of sheer fatigue and dizziness, plus mornings when she experienced burning pains on the outer sides of her knees and elbows.

The doctor continued with his message of *"It will go just like it came"* and insisted that his advice to relax was the only solution. Lisa, however, was unconvinced, so she began to make notes and to keep a personal medical diary.

This took six months before Lisa had enough data to collate the facts that the most severe bouts of what was patently IBS occurred in the days following student parties where she drank cider and cheap wine and consumed quantities of crisps and chocolate.

A medical student suggested that she might have a form of IBS related to an allergy to certain foods. She also arranged for Lisa to be seen jointly by the Head of the Faculty of Medicine and the Professor of Dietetics.

They advised a change of diet and the total avoidance of anything which might contain yeast. At first this was a disaster because the IBS inconveniences and pains became ten times worse. The academics recommended perseverance and were proved right.

On about the tenth morning, Lisa felt so good that she went jogging and played squash for the first time in two terms. In the following two weeks she had no headaches and within six weeks there was neither diarrhoea nor stomach pain.

The medics explained that the massive change in a basic element of diet had brought about a massive reaction, but it was now time for a gradual return to normal. She was counselled to begin reintroducing a few crisps and the odd half glass of wine into her life and to do the same with the other substances they had banned. Lisa was advised to keep a food diary and if there was any reaction to even small quantities of reintroduced foods, to avoid them for a further three months.

When the faculty staff used Lisa as a seminar patient study, they confessed that they had no idea what had triggered off the IBS chain of events. They could only say for certain that the stress she put herself under was altering the complex chemical balances of her body and was aggravating the problems. Picking on yeast was a bit of a guess, but you have to start somewhere.

The experts were honest enough to admit that their diagnosis of IBS was a piece of intuitive medicine inspired because there was a lack of any obvious disease or injury which could be the cause.

THE PROBLEM IS ALSO A MYSTERY

This is a common way of finding the truth. If you prove that many things are either absolutely impossible, or that they are totally non-existent, then anything which remains must be what you are looking for. Much diagnosis of IBS is similarly derived. Even in medicine, there is no substitute for experience.

Just as IBS has no one hundred per cent single definitive cause, neither does it have an assured one-off cure. The sufferer may have to explore several avenues before the truth and relief come to light. There may be fifty causes and fifty possible cures.

The comforts are that the bowel is no different from any other piece of engineering. If it breaks down it can usually be repaired and malfunction will be rectified more quickly if the patient is confident and understands what is happening.

You can begin to get this personal anti-IBS ammunition on the very next page, where we start to trace the path of food from entry to exit.

3   We Are What We Eat

The statement that 'We are what we eat' is one of those clichés which we all use from time to time. It seems to pass from our brain to our mouth with no hitches along the way. And we tend to expect our food to do the same, but – sadly – this is not always the case.

Digestion and bowels are on that list of 'not quite nice' topics of conversation and education. We can all recognise and locate the orifices at the start and finish of that process which starts with food at one end and terminates with the expulsion of waste products at the other. But how many of us have much idea of what happens to that food along the way? How many could even name the separate chambers through which it passes?

In fact, the above cliché should be amended to read that 'We are what we manage to digest'. Digestion is considerably assisted if you understand what is happening inside and so take steps to acquire good eating habits. By helping your stomach to work at its most efficient level, you will also be helping to reduce some of the IBS effects. You are getting your bowel in tune with the rest of you rather than irritating it into malfunction.

Digestion is loosely defined as that process which turns food into those other chemicals which build new muscles, repair damaged tissue, provide us with warmth and give us energy – to name but a few. Logically, a plate of chips or a steak are not much good to us in their original form, so they must be broken down into the components which the body needs. This cannot happen all at once, so the food must be conveyor-belted at a speed allowing each department to take out what it needs and then letting the raw material pass along to the next station. Eventually nothing useful remains, so the surplus is discharged.

From school biology lessons, you possibly remember that food-stuffs are generally categorised as protein, fat or carbohydrate

PROTEINS are changed into amino acids which are the products used to manufacture muscles, bone marrow, kidney tissue, liver cells, skin, hair and nails. The acids are carried to the outposts of the body by the circulating blood.

FATS have a number of functions. In their raw form they provide a certain amount of lubrication and protective layers for some organs, bones and joints. These fatty layers are an insulant providing warmth and can – if the need arises – be broken down to give energy.

CARBOHYDRATES are chemically-treated and become those vita-mins and minerals which the body uses as checks and balances to maintain 'good health'. Some carbohydrates are turned into sugar, which is the body's fuel for immediate energy and action.

When you come to think about it, that is a very clever process. We tend to eulogise the brain and are willing to talk about the heart, but the mouth, the gut and the intestines are just as sophisticated. We should give them more respect and a bit more help. If you increase your level of respect for your stomach, you straightaway help to decrease those malfunctions which irritable bowels bring.

OVERALL VIEW

In its normal passage from A-Z, food travels about 12 metres (say 40 feet) and takes about two days to make the journey.

THE MOUTH

As soon as food enters the mouth, the breaking down process begins. Obviously, the very acts of biting and chewing and grinding large masses of solid food down into smaller lumps gets the process off to a good start. But this first cavity does much more besides.

The mechanical process of chewing food, preceded by anticipation of the pleasure of eating, excites the mouth's glands to release saliva.

This has a prime function of lubricating the morsels so that they more easily slide down to the next department, but also contains an enzyme called *ptyalin*, which breaks down large lumps of starchy substance into sugars. So, even at this very early stage a chemical process is already added to the mechanical side.

An enzyme is both a 'breaking down' agent and a catalyst to speed up the chemical changes caused by other substances.

When we talk about the chewing, or the mastication of food, we begin to see a possible cause of that overlay which is indigestion and then IBS. One sort of sufferer is the overweight person who gulps food down in large lumps without chewing it the legendary 26 times. These big chunks are more difficult to break down, so the process takes longer, or is only 90 per cent completed. This irritates the bowel by making it work too hard.

The slower, longer-chewing person who is not an over-eater is really giving the digestive system much more of a chance to work. Such a person will be less likely to suffer belching, indigestion, rumbling tummy and constipation – all classic IBS inconveniences. Much preventive 'medicine' is this sort of common sense.

THE OESOPHAGUS

The oesophagus, or gullet, is a short tube of 8 inches (20 cm) or so, which does not have much of a part in actual digestion. Its sole function is to act as a transfer tube for the food to pass from mouth, via the chest cavity, to stomach.

However, even this needs some sort of motor to push the food along. It does not just drop down by gravity, otherwise bedded patients would not be able to swallow and astronauts would die of starvation.

Food is moved downstream by alternate waves of muscular contraction and relaxation – a bit like hand-squeezing sausage meat or icing along a tube-shaped bag. Some of these alternations are deliberate in the physical act of swallowing, whilst others are automatic in order to keep up the momentum.

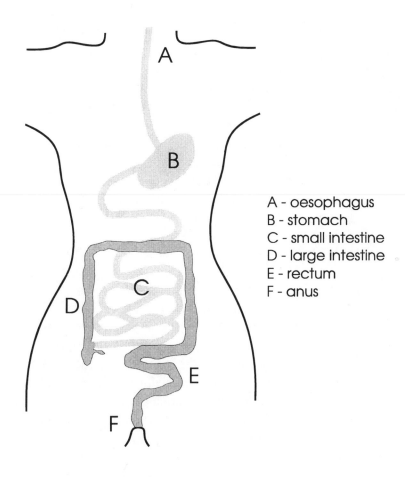

A - oesophagus
B - stomach
C - small intestine
D - large intestine
E - rectum
F - anus

The Human Digestive System

The gullet is a heavily muscled organ. In fact, it has two distinct muscular groups, or layers. To understand how they work, you should visualise a muscle as a piece of stretched elastic attached to a soft fabric. When the elastic contracts, the shape of the cloth changes.

One set of oesophagus muscles is stretched along its length. When they contract, the part they are connected to becomes shorter, fatter and more bunched. A second layer is wrapped around the tube in such a way that they give it a strong squeeze when they are made to contract.

This process of contract-then-relax is called *peristalsis*. It happens all along the digestive system. When it is functioning correctly, digestion is very smooth, but any aberrations are obviously an IBS contributor. When no food is being taken in, the very muscular oesophagus goes into total relaxation and shrinks down to a very constricted passage.

THE STOMACH

First anatomy lessons generally bring the surprise that the stomach is not actually where we rub below the waist, but tucked in behind the ribs. Food passes in via a *sphincter* – a one-way valve which opens for ingress, but will not allow material to return to the gullet.

This is very important because the contents of the stomach are extremely acid and whereas its own walls are lined with a non-corrosive layer, the walls of the oesophagus do not enjoy similar protection and can become inflamed and even mildly ulcerated if the sphincter is not closing properly.

The best way to visualise the working of the stomach is to see it as a flexible food mixer in which the contents are swirled around for 3 to 4 hours. The agitation causes big particles to break down to smaller units and the small ones to get the texture of paste. This process is considerably assisted by a complex cocktail of enzymes and acids released by the body's very sophisticated, automatic apparatus.

Movement of the food inside the stomach is caused by automatic muscular contractions, regulated by a dedicated pacemaker sending 'electrical' signals just like the one controlling the heart, to give one squeeze every 20 seconds or so.

The stomach also contains a number of micro-organisms, which is another word for tiny living creatures or bacteria. Most of these are essential to the breakdown of certain solids. The parallel here is the perfectly hygienic and efficient septic tank which is a common part of rural sewerage systems. Like a sewage farm, its efficiency partly depends on the bacteria living below the crust to neutralise many of the living and dead organisms contained in the raw material.

In addition to the bacteria which are 'on our side' and which are needed to retain good health and digestion, there are a number of 'bandit bacteria' present. As long as these are outnumbered and kept under control, they do no harm, but if they are allowed to dominate, their effects are far-reaching (even beyond the digestive tract) and are certainly a common cause of IBS.

At the end of the food mixer process, the stomach is ready to pass its contents on to the next section. At this time, the foodstuffs look like a brown version of tomato purée - ie a mixture of very tiny particles suspended in a liquid. The stomach's exit hole is controlled by the *pyloric sphincter* – another one-way valve – which will open sufficiently to allow the purée to pass, but retains any lumps until they are sufficiently broken down to move on.

THE DUODENUM

The next section of the passage is the first part of the small intestine or bowels proper. Called the duodenum, it is a 9 to 10 inch tube (25 cm approx) which does not do much to its contents apart from acting as a mixing chamber to receive the digestive assistance juices created by the gall-bladder and the pancreas. (The former adds bile to the mixture and the latter injects pancreatic acid and insulin.)

THE BOWEL – SMALL INTESTINE

So far, our food has been prepared for proper absorption. This is to say that it has been made ready and the other ingredients added, but it has not actually passed on any of its nutrients to do their fuelling, warming and healing tasks around the rest of the body.

This process is now about to begin in the small intestine which, as its name suggests, is one of two different sized food handling tubes. In fact they are much more than mere tubes because at each point along the way, they allow selected substances to pass out through their walls.

The small intestine is roughly an inch (2.5 cm) in diameter and about 20 feet – approximately 6 metres – in length. It is very neatly coiled in the centre of what the layman calls the belly, tummy or abdomen with its centre roughly behind the belly button. It is held in place by its own series of tough membranes.

Like the other tubes, the small intestine is surrounded by both longitudinal and circular muscles, whose contractions cause the contents to slide along. These are so-called smooth muscles. They are made of very fine fibres and work automatically under the control of the body's regulating computer – the central nervous system.

The food passes along the small intestine. This can take up to 48 hours. The rate of progress is dictated by very short sections of muscles around the small bowel wall giving a squeeze every 3 to 4 seconds.

En route, the contents go on being mixed with acids and enzymes, but they are also continuously in contact with a thousand little cells sticking out from the intestinal wall. These are called *villi* and can be visualised as very sensitive, very fine, hollow probes, each sucking out its chosen substance and passing it through the wall into the blood.

We shall return to this topic in more detail further on, but it is worth pointing out that if these muscular contractions (spasms) become irregular, it causes spastic gut which in turn means that you either rush to the loo at short notice, or get there and cannot perform. This is one aspect of the bowel being irritated.

THE LARGE INTESTINE (COLON)

When it passes from small to large intestine, the food has given up most of its goodness. The task now remains to take out salt and water and to prepare the waste products for expulsion. The large intestine is about 2.5 inches across (6 cm) and some 5 feet (or 1.5 metres) long. It passes up the right side of the abdomen, turns across the top and goes down the left side to join into the rectum. In appearance, it looks like a very long Michelin Man, concertina-shaped in a series of bulges and constrictions. The food can remain in the colon for up to three days.

The essential extraction of salt and water happens in a number of ways. The body is continually losing vital salt in perspiration, breath and urine – some studies suggest that a normal, working male will need to replace about 1.5 ounces of salt a day. It comes from normal food and is taken out in the large intestine. This organ also takes out over a gallon of water a day to top up the body's fluids.

The large intestine is also segmented into sections squeezing and contracting in a rhythmic movement which pushes the contents along and dries them out. At the same time, the contents are bound together into small lumps (or stools) which are held in amalgamation and externally lubricated by a mucus produced in the large bowel itself.

THE RECTUM

The final tubular section is the rectum – some 5 to 6 inches long and very elastic. This is a storeroom for prepared waste products and becomes distended as more faeces are pushed in (average contents 5 ounces/150 grams) until it has had enough and sends out a signal to be emptied. This is felt as a need to defecate.

THE BOWEL ACTION

Defecation is usually a voluntary action ie it is under the person's control. It is a muscular squeeze which forces the contents of the rectum out through the final valve or anus.

4 The Irritable Bowel Under The Microscope

By this time, you should be building up a picture of the environment in which irritable bowel syndrome can occur and beginning to get an idea of which physical and psychological types might be most at risk. However, in order to develop this picture to a level where it will be of more use to the general reader, we need to go back to the very start.

Irritable bowel is a syndrome and a syndrome is a combination of several signs and symptoms indicating a disorder. The word originates from the two Greek words *syn* and *dramein* which literally mean running together ie lots of things are happening at the same time. That is certainly very true of any IBS situation.

A symptom can be defined as any noticeable sensation or change away from normal in a person's bodily function, indicating a disease or disorder. A symptom is a sign that something is changing or happening.

WHAT IS NORMAL?

Before we can identify that the bowel is not behaving as it should, we need to know what is right or normal. Here we run into a certain amount of difficulty where even medical researchers quarrel amongst themselves.

One symptom of IBS is a change in the frequency of the patient's visits to the lavatory. Normal frequency for defecation can be anything from once every three days to four times a day. Most people empty their bowels twice a day and some are very proud of their regularity in only performing once a day and always at the same time. Equally, people like teachers get so used to using the toilet during breaks between lessons that as soon as 11 o'clock arrives their bodies are demanding the circular seat and they become very agitated if something occurs to prevent the visit.

So, the frequency of bowel movement is normal if you feel comfortable with it. However, if you reach a stage where the call of nature can never be denied, even for five minutes, you need proper medical advice.

THE NERVOUS SYSTEM

All the body's working is controlled by the brain. It passes its commands via a thick 'cable' which is the *central nervous system* in the spinal column and then along 'wires' which are the *nerves* running out to every part of the body. The signals differ very little, in fact, from those electrical and electronic messages running around inside a computer.

These messages are of two sorts. The brain can cause a deliberate action like activating (contracting) the muscles which clench the fist or turn your head.

Secondly, the brain causes things to happen completely automatically and totally outside the person's control. This occurs during exertion when the heart is ordered to speed up its rate and to circulate more oxygen-carrying blood to the muscles involved. Later, it will be told to slow down again.

Some organs can be operated both consciously and/or automatically. You can blink your eye, for instance, but it will also close of its own accord if threatened.

The smooth passage of food along from section to section of the bowel is not under conscious control. It is totally automatic and is regulated by its own form of sub-computer called the *enteric nervous system*. We have dubbed it a sub-computer because in times of great stress it is shut down by the main control centre. If you are fighting for your life, for instance, you need all that blood and energy for the main task and the last thing you want is a feeling of needing to go to the toilet. So in traumatic moments no gut/digestive activity takes place.

It gives you something of an insight into the complex physical and psychological links between IBS and stress when you realise that when you are about to do something frightening like appear in court, or make a parachute jump, it may bring about temporary diarrhoea. This also leads to even more alarming and deep-rooted bowel problems if you are consciously and subconsciously under the stress of experiencing feelings of apprehension 24 hours a day. You can well imagine the effect which such continual tension will create.

If something happens to upset the totally automatic functioning of the enteric nervous system, you are in an IBS situation. This might be a speeding up of the bowel contents mobility, a slowing down, the injection of too much of a particular acid, the reduction of the amount released of a certain enzyme, or all of these things together.

It is highly likely that minor aberrations are occurring all the time. An uncontrollable belch, the unintentional passing of wind, a burp of acidic liquid into the mouth, a tummy rumble, etc, happens to us all from time to time. It is only when they occur with great frequency and intensity that there is something to worry about.

HAVE I GOT IT?

That is the nub of the problem for sufferers: agreeing that we all show some of the symptoms of IBS at some time, when are we 'ill' enough to need to go to the doctor and will he diagnose IBS anyway?

As a rule of thumb go to the doctor when you feel apprehensive enough to be uncomfortable about your condition. If you want a more precise yardstick, book an appointment when you are experiencing a number of the symptoms and feelings below.

SIGNS AND SYMPTOMS

- Frequent but irregular stomach pain, generally quite low down in the abdomen but can be either side or centre.
- Diarrhoea, possibly also with abdominal pain.
- Constipation, almost always with some stomach ache or pain in the rectal area.
- Alternating bouts of diarrhoea and constipation. Time span varies and can be erratic.
- Stomach which constantly feels bloated and stretched to maximum capacity following just a light meal, or even no meal at all.
- Feeling that the stomach is full of trapped wind.
- Stools which are very hard. 'Rabbit droppings' syndrome.
- Passing mucus either on its own or between stools.
- Very constant tummy rumbling.
- Very frequent belching.
- Very embarrassing frequent flatulence.

It will often happen that these symptoms will lie low for a while, then reappear, or increase if the sufferer is put under even minor stress. This could be something like a row with a partner, a forthcoming important/disagreeable interview, or anxiety about the bank balance towards the end of the salary month.

Some IBS patients also complain of one or several of the side-effects in the list below.

Heartburn, occasional sickness, foul tasting mouth, diminished appetite, inability to concentrate, nausea, problems with swallowing, acid taste in mouth, lethargy, depression.

There is often neither rhyme nor rhythm to attacks of these side-effects and even doctors are often unsure of whether they are caused by IBS or cause it. The actual reasons for their occurrence can also be difficult or impossible to isolate. Even more mystifying is why many IBS sufferers also experience backache, headaches accompanied by perspiration and even a burning feeling in some joints.

Women are likely to suffer the extra irritants of hot flushes, difficult menstruation and experience pain during sexual intercourse. This causes anxiety which is reflected by an increase in all the irritating conditions already listed. We shall discuss these physical and mental interactions more fully in chapter five, but here it should be reiterated that worry is one of the main causes of IBS.

Doctors report that the cancer and ulcer bogeys crop up in the minds of many patients who observe that:

- They occasionally pass mucus – a more frequent occurrence with age.
- They can see and recognise unabsorbed food in their stools.
- They have constant tummy rumblings and other noises.
- They see an occasional spot of blood in stools.

It cannot be repeated too often that there is absolutely no known connection between the relatively minor traumas of IBS and a disease as serious as cancer, but that if you have any changes in your normal patterns, you must visit your doctor.

THE CAUSES

In the case of IBS the cause could be something recognisably physical such as:

- Injury or operation.
- Reaction to a bout of gastro enteritis, Spanish holiday tummy, or gastric flu.
- After-effects of the medicines used to cure the above ie a drug can inhibit/increase the flow of a particular enzyme or hormone and this in turn upsets the digestion for a while.

Equally, a group of causes could be related to personality and the effects of circumstances on a person's 'psyche'. By this we mean divorce, work problems, the change of life, money worries, exams, threats of redundancy, children's behaviour, etc. These are the causes where (unavoidably in most cases) we bring IBS upon ourselves.

WHO CAN GET IBS?

The short answer to this is just about anybody, with the rider that we will all experience some of the symptoms on occasions. If these occasional appearances become frequent, then it is time to consult your doctor and to hide nothing from him.

"DOCTOR, I THINK I'VE GOT IBS – OR SOMETHING"

It takes much more courage to go along to the doctor to discuss a complaint in a part of the body which you cannot see, than to seek help for a boil or a bruise. Seeking help for IBS-related problems is also delayed because many people are very shy about talking of their toilet habits. In some cases they are terrified because they do not know the polite, or medical words to describe these facts and functions.

The fears are groundless. Doctors are used to such communication problems. They are also aware that the idea of being subjected to tests – especially involving a visit to a hospital – makes some patients almost paralysed with apprehension – and that in turn exacerbates the IBS symptoms.

If either you or your doctor suspect IBS, he will almost certainly spend some time asking plenty of questions. Some of these might seem unrelated to you because they are wider ranging than the physical maladies which you are suffering. The doctor is here trying to get a patient history, a picture of a life and health style which might throw up a cause. The conversation will almost certainly range over food, drugs and your personal toilet habits and experiences.

The prime purpose of this initial consultation will be to determine that you are not suffering from something more serious than an irritation. To be totally sure of this the doctor will possibly make a preliminary rectal examination by inserting a gloved finger into the anal orifice to test the freeness of the passage and the health of the muscular wall. He might ask for a sample stool to be sent for analysis or even to extract a specimen himself.

If this manual examination is inconclusive, the next step might be a *sigmoidoscopy*. Its object is to make a visual examination of the inside of the large bowel and it is accomplished by a small medical telescope which has a light at the end. The sigmoidoscope is gently inserted into the rectum. This is not a very painful procedure because modern machines use fibre optics which basically allow light and images to be bent around corners. These new medical tools are smaller, finer and most efficient.

Some local medical centres have their own means for this sort of diagnosis, but smaller practices might need to use the equipment at a local hospital. No matter where you are examined, there is no need to fear a sigmoidoscopy because about 95 per cent of the examinations do no more than give the patient a clean bill of health. The other five per cent may need a further, more detailed examination.

The final elimination test might possibly be a *barium enema*. This takes a bit more time and generally begins with a mild laxative the night before to ensure a bowel action before the test. The doctor will then inject a small amount of fluid containing barium into the rectum. This shows up on X-rays and enables the experts to confirm that there is nothing wrong inside the gut. A barium enema is a relatively painless process and generally has no side-effects other than mild flatulence for a few hours.

Your doctor might do all these tests, or you might be sent to the hospital for some of them. They could well be spread over a couple of weeks. In most cases they confirm that there is nothing organically, seriously wrong with the patient, so the symptoms will be put on the medical record under the IBS umbrella and a search begun to find their root-cause.

THE THEORIES

Finding the cause is where the problem really starts. Most IBS patients are not really 'ill' in the normal understanding of the word, but neither are they one hundred per cent fit. So a cure has to be found even if there is no single discernible cause.

As briefly discussed, the basic malaise could be any one of the theories below, or it could be a combination of any of them. It should be emphasised that 'theories' is a well-chosen word, even though the ideas are guided by experience.

The *aftermath of a more serious disease* like gastro-enteritis, or even the antibiotics used in its cure, is a possible cause. *Mild food poisoning* which seems to have cured itself can also leave a lasting effect on the gut ie cause it to be deficient in certain necessary enzymes and acids which are used to break down food, or to make it firm enough for comfortable expulsion.

Symptoms could also be caused by a lack of some of the *hormones* the body needs. A hormone is a chemical produced by glands inside the body and has a specific job to do.

Muscular disorder is believed to be a very common IBS cause. Roughly speaking it means that something is causing the clocks which control the interior muscle contractions to speed up or to slow down. These in turn cause diarrhoea and constipation. The reasons for 'clock failure' are very baffling and the subject of very serious research. The cure might only be effected by trial and error and a great deal of patience.

Fibre deficiency is often cited as the main cause of IBS. In a nutshell, it means that the patient's diet lacks enough of what used to be called roughage which is supplied by leafy vegetables, fruits and bran. These foodstuffs are chiefly valued because they contain pectin, which is used to cause jam to set firm, plus lignin, which is what causes plant stems and parsnip cores to get their woody qualities. If you have loose bowel actions, increasing your inake of high-fibre foods will obviously do no harm.

Food intolerance is a very wide study in its own right. It can range over why some children are not able to absorb nitrogen and suffer apparent lowered intelligence symptoms, right through to why the author is totally unable to eat certain types of Breton crêpes without almost immediate vomiting, diarrhoea and dizziness.

We eat so many foods that it might take your doctor quite a while to isolate the one, or the combination, which is causing your IBS problems. Logically, this can be one area where a large degree of patient self-help is possible.

Lactose intolerance falls into the same category. It is still only a theory because it is not totally understood, but cutting out milk, cheese, yoghurt and chocolate from a diet can also cut out many of the IBS effects. Such exclusion is one of those cure methods which might work or might not.

Mental problems would be high on the list of IBS culprits. The range of things causing worry, stress and other mental irritants and disorders is huge. This is a study which is as fascinating as it is complex.

We shall try to explain this mental and physical action, reaction and interaction in an ordinary person's language in the next chapter.

5 Mental Or Physical?

In writing this chapter, I am conscious of stepping into a minefield where not only are all the experts unsure of where the mines are located, but neither do they have precise knowledge about the types of mine, or even if they exist in harmful form.

Before taking our first steps, there are a few questions which we should ask ourselves:

1. Do we consider that the brain can influence the body enough to cause pain or disorder even when there is no disease or other obvious physical damage present?
2. Do we consider that a physical problem can influence the mind ie cause depression, forgetfulness or hyperactivity?
3. Is there a ping-pong ball effect of the mind causing a body illness, then worry about this problem, giving rise to even more exaggerated physical symptoms, which in turn increase the tension, anxiety, depression, stress, etc to disturb the mind?
4. Could this pendulum, or chain reaction, be triggered off by a physical effect?

Put even more simply, we are asking ourselves whether IBS can be caused by a mental disturbance (however slight) or do the physical maladies of diarrhoea and constipation cause the brain to be over-active in some respects. Maybe we have a chicken and egg situation here. Which comes first – the mental tension or the IBS symptoms? Which is the cause and which is the effect?

If you are confused about this, so are many doctors and medical scientists. There is much evidence to support the so-called psychological theorists and an equal amount to support the physical cause protagonists. It may well be that both sides are right and that two people suffering the same type of IBS effects might have contracted them from different sources. One person may be embarrassed by acute diarrhoea brought on by nervous tension and the stress of a financial crisis. A second might suffer constipation because his bowel muscles have been slowed down by the spin-off from a drug administered – say – as a pain killer for tennis elbow, or by sleep-inducing tablets.

Before we come down on one side or the other, or indeed take up the centre and admit that both sides could be right, it will be of assistance to refresh our knowledge of how the brain controls the body and – reciprocally – is influenced by it.

THE NERVOUS SYSTEMS

THE CENTRAL NERVOUS SYSTEM controls all our voluntary movements. It is mostly under our control but can be totally paralysed in times of terror or panic. Its willingness and ability to tell muscles to do things can also be reduced by seemingly unconnected events.

An office worker who has been sitting in a chair all day, but using his brain in overdrive can feel physically very tired. Something is telling these unworked muscles that they are exhausted, so cannot perform the required task with enthusiasm.

THE AUTOMATIC NERVOUS SYSTEM controls all the body systems not under our purposeful control. The speed of heartbeat, perspiration and the rate at which food is moved through the digestive system are the prime examples.

Yet the physical act of eating a substance that your body does not like, or the mental sensation of being afraid can upset all these rhythms. You can even perspire when you are freezing cold.

THE SYMPATHETIC NERVOUS SYSTEM is generally responsible for speeding up these automatic functions in response to stimuli. The sweat glands open if your temperature goes up, extra blood is brought to a bad bruise and your heart rate increased to supply it.

THE PARASYMPATHETIC NERVOUS SYSTEM is the calming agent

and the automatic mechanism which tells your heart to slow down when the panic subsides, or it shuts off the adrenaline glands when your need to compete has departed.

A malfunction in any of these systems could bring on any number of the IBS inconveniences. Equally, prolonged, heavy flatulence can cause you to worry about it if you have to attend a meeting. Perhaps you fear that your constantly rumbling tummy will ruin an intimate evening and ruin a date that you really want to be a success. So your heart rate speeds up a bit and you begin to perspire a little and get even more butterflies in your tummy just by worrying about it.

DO I REALLY WANT TO KNOW?

All these things are explained in some detail to illustrate just how difficult it can be for your doctor not so much to diagnose that you are suffering one of the many forms of IBS, but for him to identify, to isolate and to remove what could be the prime cause. This might be psychological or physiological.

The more we discuss this action, reaction and interaction between the mental and the somatic, the more we might see a gleam of comprehending light in the murky muddle and so we will increase our chances of giving the doctor some helpful information. The more we understand ourselves and how we function, the clearer and more numerous are our possibilities for helping ourselves: for finding something which eases the irritating effects. Some of these causes might go back a long way.

The Story Of Samantha

Samantha hated school because she was a very slow learner. She had plenty of parental back-up and was herself desperately keen to learn. This was not enough and the poor child was very upset at being constantly typecast as mentally inferior to her classmates, or being held in ridicule when asked to read aloud, or to reply to a spoken question in class.

Sam found that pretending to have an aching tummy usually meant that her mother allowed her to stay home for the day. This deception was maintained for about ten years until our young lady left school at sixteen and went to work in an office. It was a good job with a friend of her father.

At work, some days were good and some bad – like most jobs. The worst days were the monthly accounts, the stocktaking and the board meeting. Sam – now mistress of her own destiny – found that when she knew that a particularly vexing day was coming up, she actually developed a nasty stomach pain, so had to stay home for the day.

The tummy trouble gave rise to the further maladies of bad constipation and bloating and extremely difficult menstrual periods.

With her engagement pending, Samantha sought advice from a doctor who happened to be on the IBS wavelength. By long and careful questioning, she was able to put together the full story of how Samantha's problems were the physical manifestations of what was purely a mental and emotional problem – ie an inability to cope with the intellectual demands of certain days at work.

Our doctor also pulled a few strings and found Sam a job as a dental practice receptionist. The duties were no more onerous than booking appointments, filing records and talking to patients. The job was mentally undemanding but still fitted Sam's middle-class image.

In two years she has not taken a day off, the bloated stomach and painful periods are a thing of the past, and Sam is now happy.

The Story Of Michael

Mike is a music teacher at a school where the Head is a very bullying man who sees music, drama and other 'non-core' subjects as of little value. He let it be known that he thought Michael's department superfluous and so kept it on a low budget.

This parsimony deprived the department of the newest books and musical equipment and limited our subject's ability to produce good lessons. The pupils complained and so did their parents. The Head harangued his junior colleague in public and would frequently arrange cover for other absent teachers by cancelling the music timetable and giving Mike double classes for community singing in the school hall.

This was a disaster for discipline and morale, leading to even more complaints from the Head about Michael's professional competence.

Strangely, Michael had been one of the best students of his year at college and was apparently destined for a bright promotional career. He is also a big man and had played second row for the university rugby fifteen.

Yet this admirable man became almost a recluse because he developed all the embarrassing facets of IBS. This showed as acute swings from constipation to diarrhoea so demanding that he sometimes needed to leave in mid-lesson. That occasioned more pupil ribaldry and more confrontations with authority.

More worrying was the pain Mike was getting in his piano playing fingers. He also became more depressed about getting to hate a job he liked and in which he was ambitious for promotion.

It took Michael's doctor about three months to guess the real cause. His advice was that Mike should dig out his glowing college records and that he should talk to colleagues in other schools about the size of their budgets and the way they were treated. He was advised to write all these things down into a fact sheet.

On one traumatic day when the Head was putting his music man into the prison of a hundred pupils unable to go to games because of absent staff, Mike told the Head in front of all the staff that he wanted to see him in his office. Now!

There he towered over his boss, verbally browbeat him with all the written evidence he had collected and demanded parity of purse and possibility with music teachers in other schools. He forcefully told the boss what an idiot the staff as a whole thought him to be and also let it be known that he was not going to leave the school, but was willing to put his case before the full governing body, the County Director of Education, Her Majesty's Regional Inspector of Music, his union representative and his family solicitor. All this was done in a noise loud enough for the Head's secretary to hear in the next room. It was accompanied by a great deal of strong language and desk banging.

In that school, the story of how Mike went back to playing rugby and did them all a favour by beating a tyrant into line is cause for an annual lunchtime drink. Only Michael knows that he has a second drink to celebrate vanishing bowel complaints and the return of supple fingers.

The Story Of Joan

Joan had been practically housebound for two years because of her fear of being caught at a distance from a toilet which she used very frequently.

Whilst her husband was working away, Joan received the telephoned news that her twelve-year-old son had fallen badly from his cycle at the end of the road and had been lying there for almost an hour, but the ambulance had not yet turned up.

Scared, Joan drove the family car for the first time in two years and took her son the ten miles to the nearest casualty department. There she stayed with him for three hours to receive first aid, visit the X-ray department and to see a second doctor.

It was only when she had driven home again and made her son comfortable in bed with a light meal, that she realised that she had not given a visit to the toilet a single thought for the past five hours.

IBS MENTAL OR PHYSICAL?

The above instances have been related in some detail to illustrate the problems your doctor might have in diagnosing IBS, or which particular part of the syndrome might be causing your illness. To establish the root-cause, he will need help and you will need patience. After all, it is comparatively easy to appreciate how acute diarrhoea, or frequent stomach rumbling and flatulence in public, can cause the emotional sub-maladies of tension, nervousness and perspiration. It is, however, less easy to get a picture of why an impending exam, or being visited by the police, or a bad bank statement should cause diarrhoea or any of the other physical ailments of irritable bowel.

Then remember our nervous systems. If the muscles of your gut are getting confused messages because your central computer is heavily committed to a worrying task, it becomes clearer how the mental has an effect on the physical.

A syndrome is a set of symptoms and a symptom is the body's way of telling you that there is something wrong so you had better think about doing something to put it right; in most cases this means seeing a doctor.

However, before the visit, use the knowledge you now have and write down a list of the things which might be significant. Problems at home? The mortgage? Work worries? Personal cash flow? Been using laxatives?

If you can help your doctor, he will be able to help you and even help you to help yourself by some of the cures we discuss next.

6   How The Doctor Helps

In this next section we shall tell you about some of the cures which your doctor might prescribe for IBS. This is not to pre-empt his method of cure, nor to persuade you to help yourself with no aid other than yourself. Whilst it is true that there are many common sense steps which you can take to relieve parts of IBS (we shall cover them in chapter nine), the fact remains that the safest and surest way to rid yourself of the inconvenience, anguish and embarrassment of bowel problems is to let the professionals sort it out.

So, there are three reasons for writing this chapter on what the doctor might suggest:

1.   To persuade you to book that first appointment because you need it.
2.   To explain to you that the treatments are – for the most part – neither very arduous nor very uncomfortable.
3.   So that you and the doctor will have some common ground. Hopefully, you will speak the same language and you will be a better and more conscientious patient because you understand what your healer is trying to do.

There are critics (some of them doctors) who decry the idea of a patient understanding part of their mystique. They scream that *"a little learning is a dangerous thing"*. This is nonsense. The man who understands how his car works is not necessarily going to try to repair it. Usually he has neither the tools and the spare parts nor the really practical skills to do it. He can, however, better explain what is wrong and will more gratefully understand what the engineer is doing to repair the fault.

Just as our knowledgeable car owner will understand how the

vehicle fault occurred and can take precautions against such future neglect, so it is with the patient. When your doctor weaves his magic to make all your IBS ills vanish, your knowledge will help you to make those minor lifestyle changes which are necessary to ensure that they do not return.

WHICH ROUTE WILL YOUR DOCTOR TAKE?

The cures for IBS obviously depend on the causes. Mostly, there is no single discernible reason for bowel malfunction, so your doctor might prescribe several elements of one of the curative series below, or he might see the answer as a combination of healants from more than one of them.

In general terms, there are three possible healing routes to take:

1. The pills and potions route of clinically-controlled chemicals – drugs and medicines – designed to strengthen your body's weaknesses and to kill off the things which have either upset the balance by becoming too powerful, or which should not be there in the first place.

2. The dietary method of changing the foods we eat to remove or to cut down those which are causing the bowels to behave abnormally.

3. The relaxation and mental change road which sees IBS as stress (even boredom) related and which works along the lines of 'a change is as good as a rest'. We could actually alter that to say that 'a rest is as good as a change' and might well do some good if you are under pressure.

IBS AND MEDICINES

If your doctor decides that your particular form of IBS needs to be cured by ingested medicines, there are a number of possible options. But, before talking about specific examples, we need to have a general knowledge of what we are talking about.

Medicines, antibiotics and drugs all tend to get lumped together by non-medical experts, with 'drugs' nowadays having many unsavoury connotations. The dictionary definitions are interesting.

MEDICINE – a drug or remedy used in treating, preventing and alleviating the symptoms of a disease or injury.

ANTIBIOTIC – a chemical substance such as penicillin, streptomycin or tetracycline produced naturally by micro-organisms and fungi, but also produced synthetically for the destruction and inhibition of the growth of such other micro-organisms as bacteria and similar carriers and causes of disease and illness.

DRUG – a natural or man-made chemical substance used in the cure, prevention and analysis of disease. (The secondary meaning of a drug to describe a narcotic, or other substance consumed for the pleasant effect it produces, is obviously not part of our brief.)

So, when your doctor speaks of giving you a medicine, an antibiotic or a curative drug, he might be talking very precisely, but we can lump the terms together as different varieties of a healing agent.

IS IT REAL?

It is an unavoidable part of modern society that we almost expect to be treated by drugs. It is interesting to reflect that Man is the only animal curing himself of ills in this way. In fact, we have so much come to expect a rapid cure by the easy route of 'popping a pill' that many patients first approach their doctor with the suggestion *"Doctor, can you give me something for . . . ?"*

If you go with that approach, you will probably be offered some-thing, even if it is only a placebo, or harmless, neutral substance. If you think that this lump of coated sugar is doing you good, then you will probably notice an improvement.

There is an old cliché – that the patient pays the doctor to amuse him, whilst Nature cures the complaint. This is not true of all IBS maladies, but there is a strong school of thought that 90 per cent of bowel irritations are best cured by natural methods. But for these you need patience.

This approach to medicine was beautifully reinforced to me by a pharmacist friend whom I had approached for a chemico-heat cream to treat a muscular injury incurred by an over enthusiastic squash match. When I asked him what I was paying for, he thought for a moment and said, *"When you come to people like me, you are mostly buying time. Use the jelly, but do not be in too much of a hurry to start playing again."*

There is also the medical dictum that *"Show me a drug which does not have a side-effect and I will show you one which is not doing the patient any good."*

This is why your doctor might ask you to come back in a week's time before he will offer you a prescription. He might suggest a minor change in your daily routine, but he will possibly also wish to consider the options in relation to your medical history. If you have been using a contraceptive pill, or been on a course of sleeping pills or even regularly using milk of magnesia, he will want to be very sure that what he prescribes will work well with no spin-off discomforts and no interference with other treatments.

Since the huge thalidomide scandal, there has also developed a strong patient resistance to drugs of any sort. If you belong to the 'natural cures' school of thought, you need to overcome this reluctance. The drugs and medicines trade is a vast financial empire which does actually commit a large proportion of its budget to making itself the most carefully controlled, tested and regulated industry in the world.

Here, we should also make the point that a doctor will have open to him a number of drug options for the same effect. That is, there will be several compounds which do roughly the same things, so most doctors stick to a relatively small group of drugs for each illness. These are antibiotics which they know well and with which they have had excellent results. From experience they will know the exact strength and frequency to suit you as an individual.

There is no substitute for experience, so if you go to a doctor and he suggests a chemical cure, believe me, he will almost always be right. So you too must believe this. The drugs route to the alleviation of IBS has a number of trunk roads according to major symptoms.

TELL THE GUT TO SLOW DOWN

ANTISPASMODIC DRUGS are designed to slow down the number of times per minute which the gut's muscles contract, or to diminish the strength and intensity of this contraction. You will doubtless recall the way in which the smooth muscles grouped along the tubes and around them shorten, or contract, to squeeze food along their length.

How muscles are actually told to contract and what causes contraction is another of those vastly complicated biological processes which are still not one hundred per cent understood.

However, what is clear is that our autonomic nervous system passes electrical impulse signals down nerve 'wires' which get progressively finer until they reach the nerve ends. These ends are separated from the actual muscle fibre (there are hundreds of these per square inch and they all contract) by a space. At the arrival point, the electrical signal has to jump a gap – a bit like a spark plug.

In the case of the muscle, the gap is filled with a variety of chemicals. The electrical signal tells the gap how much of what chemical to pump out and to pass on to tiny organs called receptors, which are actually on the muscle fibre. Only certain molecules can attach to the receptor, so it does not normally make mistakes. If all is going well, the muscles contract at their natural rhythm and digestion and defecation are efficient, comfortable and normal.

If an irritating food, or a contaminant in the blood upsets this chemical transfer agency, the muscular rhythm can change. Your doctor will probably prescribe a chemical (drug) to restore the situation.

THIS WILL BE AN ANTISPASMODIC. The drug path to an IBS cure should be trodden with cautious optimism. Because IBS is a group of complaints with probably a group of causes, there is no instant panacea. There is still much work to be done on an umbrella curative drug. Until it is developed, 'Try it and see' might have to be the motto.

On the credit side, if stomach pain is the main symptom, drugs have a good record. They can also control diarrhoea and constipation in the short-term. They are less certain to produce a complete cure for this pair of irritants together, so the final solution might have to be sought elsewhere.

IS IT IN MY MIND?

As in most IBS related ideas, the question *"Is it in my mind?"* is too simple. If there is no apparent physical cause for this disturbing set of symptoms, the answer might well be *"Yes, it is in your mind and in your personality and in the general way you conduct you life, or the malady could even be triggered off by the way you are being carried along by events in your life."*

Remember Mike, our cured music teacher. In this case, your doctor might prescribe the type of drug which, for want of a better phrase, works on your personality – your psyche.

The generic name for this group of medicines is psychoactive drugs, of which the most usual are the low power tranquillisers. Valium seems to be the most common and the best understood. The function of such drugs is to calm you down, to stop you from constantly discharging nervous energy in worry, to slow down your whole metabolism in an attempt to let the bowel re-find its natural pace and rhythm. The logic of this treatment is easy to comprehend.

If such drugs are prescribed in heavier doses, they send you to sleep, but your doctor will only take this course with reluctance and over a short period. Becoming dependent on these artificial aids is outside this study, but it is not uncommon.

There is also a group of drugs known as anti-depressants. They do exactly what their name implies and pep you up a bit. These are not strong drugs and there is little danger that the user will become dependent on them. Their main function is to give you a greater feeling of well-being and that in itself is a super first step towards telling IBS that you are fed up with being a victim.

The final drug method which your doctor might use smacks of grandmother and black medicine. Peppermint oil and chlorodyne are prescribed for everything from coughs and diarrhoea to flatulence and constipation for the simple reason that they appear to work. The same can be said for prescribed kaolin and codeine.

IS IT WHAT I EAT?

When relating the cure of IBS – or even its theoretical cause – to diet, we enter a world which seems to be as much governed by fashion as by medical science. If you follow the popular press, it seems that every known food ever eaten or drunk can cause cancer, impotency, indigestion and loss of memory. The next day it seems that those same foods have the reverse effect.

Totally honest analysis would also indicate that many people who are excellent physicians are not very adventurous in experimenting with food cures.

Everything is either bad for you – or good. The use of such fibre as bran is a typical example of medical fact and fad. It used to be in fashion, then it went out of fashion and is now back in favour as part of the vegetarian and natural foods wave of popularity. There are, however, several good medical reasons why your doctor might pre-scribe a high fibre diet such as we have previously touched on. Here it should be mentioned that one theory is that coarse fibre acts a bit like a wire brush and actually cleans the inner surface of the gut as it passes along. We shall discuss diet in chapter nine.

Very few doctors have sufficient time to monitor a programme of dietary change. The food intolerance school of thought is a very valid one arguing that we all at some time eat certain foods which do not agree with us. Our tolerance and intolerance might even change with time.

The only way to recognise which foods cause you problems is to stop eating certain things and to notice the effects of their absence.

The process does need time-consuming observation. If you feel that your IBS is related to your inability to ingest certain foods and you wish to undertake a series of trials, discuss this treatment with your doctor. Seek his guidance and incorporate his advice into our self-help plan of chapter ten.

In the end, like Omar Khayyam:

Myself when young did eagerly frequent
Doctor and Saint, and heard great argument
About it and about: but evermore
Came out by the same Door as in I went

We should never forget that there are millions of IBS sufferers worldwide. The degree of suffering varies from slight to serious but only you know whether you want to fight it or live with it.

If you fight, as fight you must, your two best soldiers are your doctor and yourself. In many instances you may unwittingly have brought the irritable bowel disaster on yourself. In all instances – even under medical guidance – the speed and effectiveness of the cure will be very much influenced by your own thoughts, attitudes and actions.

7 The Role Of Stress

Here we come to the big one. Stress is without any doubt the largest contributing factor either to the development of IBS or to it becoming more serious. Sometimes, stress can help to trigger off those malfunctions and imbalances which lead to a collection of symptoms, which have been lurking in the background. Also, worrying about diarrhoea and being anxious lest it proves to be something more serious, can cause tensions and other mental niggles which persuade the IBS maladies to become even worse.

Irritable bowel does not have a monopoly here. A large percentage of all other illnesses treated by doctors contain an element of stress in one form or another. The topic is so wide and so deep that we could (and probably will) devote a whole book to the subject. However, for the moment, we must all be aware of the power of tension. Simply put, stress ties up and stifles so many of our body's resources and upsets so many of our balances that it is not really surprising that the effects will show up somewhere.

WHAT IS STRESS?

The condition which we call stress, or being under intense pressure, is a bit like the proverbial elephant in being much easier to recognise than to define. In fact, it is often easier to observe in other people than to perceive in ourselves. If somebody very close to you changes their habits, clams up a bit and is less chatty, you soon get to ask what is worrying them. Plain old, simple worry is about ninety per cent of what we mean by stress.

We tend to recognise stress in friends by making such gossipy remarks as *"Tom is hitting the bottle a bit"* or *"I see Dick is chain smoking these days"* or *"Harriet is in a permanent frump. I wonder what's getting at her?"* Our comments are all about what is happening on the outside: IBS might well be what is happening on the inside.

POSITIVE OR NEGATIVE

Unfortunately, there are some similarities between the chemical changes which occur to get us fired up to solve a short-term problem and those which occur over a long period of time. In the short-term, we can get a shot of adrenaline when we are about to win a sporting tournament, or to cope with winning the football pools. We can get on a high, or receive a bit of a buzz over any number of happenings on a daily basis.

Physiologically, there is not too much difference between this happy sort of buzz and the way the brain and body gear themselves up to deal with a short-lived crisis. This is the so-called 'fight or flight effect' which concentrates the mind and gives the body extra strength whether you are protecting yourself from potential muggers, or giving chase to them.

This sort of physical/mental acceleration has no long-term ill effect on either body or brain and the parasympathetic nervous system soon takes over to slow the heart, shut off the adrenaline and take away the perspiration. At the conclusion of the fight or flight, you might feel an urgent need to visit the toilet, or your tummy might rumble, but these side-effects will disappear in minutes or hours rather than days and they are not damaging.

The more serious form of stress and the one which is most likely to aggravate diarrhoea etc, is rarely physical, but more likely to be some sort of nagging worry which is always there 'in the back of my mind' and which never seems to leave you alone. Every time your brain is unoccupied you think about the problem. Sometimes you are half thinking about it when you should be concentrating on something else. Very often it will not let you go to sleep.

This is a particularly debilitating sort of stress whose effects accumulate over a period of time and will almost always show as some form of bowel disorder which keeps on recurring.

LONG-TERM STRESS

The most common way of recognising that something is bugging you is when you say to yourself *"I feel tense"* or *"I'm getting a bit uptight about the size of my overdraft"*. It is the length of the period which does the damage. It equates to running the car engine in neutral for countless hours, or winding a spring up so tight for so long that it either snaps, or it will not return to its original untensioned shape.

When the body is tense for too long, most individuals have their own monitor that something is not right. We all have our own weak spots where the problem first shows up.

At one time, my own indicator that I had been doing/worrying too much would show as a boil on my back. After a few years teaching physical education and French, when I used my voice in a projected forte for five hours every day, stress showed as a very sore throat and a loss of voice. Since I gave up teaching, a period of worry has caused the weakness to move elsewhere and show as one or more IBS manifestations.

In this I am relatively normal in that my weak spot is located in that delicate, delicately balanced part of the body which converts food into – literally – the hundreds of separate substances and combinations of substances which a body needs to survive. The more complex a machine the higher the likelihood and the actual incidence of breakdown. If that machine is also as lightly built as the bowel, that incidence becomes even higher still.

This kind of stress can be home-related, work-inspired, or caused by any number of personal foibles related to personality and how our personality reacts to circumstances and situations which are not always totally of our own making.

You will certainly recognise something of yourself in the three types of reaction shown by three different characters faced with an annoying person who has probably cheated them of money, or been the cause of a minor car crash.

TYPE A will rant and rave with probably plenty of bad language and a great deal of arm waving and threatening gestures. Their face will probably redden and the pulse rate will increase very rapidly.

This is the classic choleric case. The word also means bilious, so in addition to working themselves towards a heart attack, Type A will not escape a long lasting bout of IBS.

TYPE B is the exact opposite. They have the reputation for being a pushover – wimpish – or even just having no emotions. Type B will always take flight rather than fight and will bottle all the rages, hurts and disappointments up inside. The emotions will stay there for a very long time, but they will never leave Type B alone. Much of their mental energy will be devoted to going over the incident a hundred times and with each repeat the bile returns to their mouth, they breathe a bit on the shallow side and get tense again.

Type B is probably doing more to cause self-inflicted (or personality inflicted) IBS than they realise. The malady is likely to be serious and prolonged.

TYPE C falls between these two extremes. Their response to the situation will be an exterior of utter calm and politeness. They will meet the challenge, but their reply will be delivered without shouting and will possibly contain a touch of sarcasm. Type C's face will generally lose some of its colour for a short while and they will usually ask for time to think about the problem, but will not let this be their priority. Type C will finally make a decision which might be a bit vengeful, but once they have acted they will feel better and the incident will be forgotten.

Even though many lucky people are born as Type C, many of their best traits of character can be deliberately inculcated. You can make yourself slow down. Remember our sacked executive and our sportsman. Their mottos – actually pinned up in large letters on the wall – were *"Don't get mad, get even"* and *"Stay cool, Boy, stay cool."*

Type C people would approve of these. Unlike A and B they are unlikely to contract any long lasting stress-related IBS symptoms.

THE SEVEN AGES. WHEN DOES STRESS OCCUR?

Question *"Does stress and stress-related IBS occur at any particular points in our lives?"*

Answer *"No"*. If you think about your own life and the lives of people you know, stress and tension can occur at any age. The cause will be different, but the symptoms and effects will be the same.

Stress can occur in:

SMALL CHILDREN who get into a paddy over something trivial. They cry, stamp their feet and clench their fists – all signs of hypertension. The fits are generally short-lived, but experienced parents will also recollect that there is generally an associated, brief, tummy or toilet problem.

ADOLESCENCE is a particularly stressful time. It is a period of acne, sports, exams and exam results, blushing, boyfriends/girlfriends, apprehension about wearing spectacles, the scramble to find a college place and to get a job. Adolescence is also a time of great healing resilience. Attacks of stress-related IBS are not likely to be long lasting.

EARLY ADULTHOOD is probably a time of getting married, getting a mortgage, having children, working up the job ladder, always needing more money and changing a lifestyle to adapt to others. These are all causes of stress.

MIDDLE THIRTIES PLUS is the make or break time for many careers. the Seven Year Itch, *"Hell I'm forty"*. Giving up some sports. The spreading waistline. This is probably the period of greatest marital, sexual and financial anxiety. This partly accounts for why the highest incidence of IBS occurs between 40 and 60 years of age.

THE SENIOR CITIZEN worries about the change of life, minor aches and pains, loneliness and abandonment, accident proneness, diminished memory, long-term illness and general ability to cope. The stress here is less strongly felt, less immediate, but very real.

UNDER STRESS? ME? HOW DO YOU KNOW?

The best way to avoid stress-related IBS is to recognise when you are getting into the wrong sort of tension and to force yourself to do something about it.

Count up to ten. Walk away from the annoying idiot. Just pretend to listen. Take a few long, slow, deep breaths.

If you are showing any of the signs below, you are moving into stress mode and it will not be too long before your bowel will begin to react.

SELF-ANALYSIS

We can all recognise when our habits change and we are doing things which would normally be alien to our nature, or things of which we would disapprove in others. The following list is what you should be looking for in yourself:
- Overeating.
- Loss of interest in food.
- Driving the car very badly – too fast and without proper care.
- Insomnia.
- Staying in bed when you are wide awake.
- Constantly drumming fingers and tapping toes.
- Higher incidence of stupid little accidents.
- Disinterest in work.
- No sexual appetite.
- Drinking and smoking more than usual.
- Biting your nails.
- Licking your lips.

THE BODY'S OWN SIGNS OF STRESS

In addition to these indicators, the body lets you know you are under stress by sending out a series of sub signals:
- The IBS diarrhoea, constipation group.

- Sudden pains in stomach, chest or neck, often for no apparent reason.
- Suddenly realising that you have been holding your breath.
- Breathing fast and shallow.
- Dry mouth and foul tasting mouth.
- Menstrual pains and problems.
- Sweating without apparent cause.
- Jumping at normal sounds – eg telephone.

THE KNOCK-ON SIGNS

All the above contribute to making you feel that you are not yourself. They are all stress signs which can affect your feelings about yourself. It all adds up to a loss of confidence. You are feeling a bit let down and slobby, so this comes out in other ways:
- Being over-sensitive to slight criticism.
- Loss of ability to concentrate.
- Constantly and even deliberately day-dreaming about more pleasant times.
- Periods of worry about trivia and minor happenings.
- Feeling inadequate and much undervalued by colleagues.
- Being unwilling to discuss problems with others.
- Untypical anger and irritability, especially with those close to you.
- A general feeling of *"I'm fed up with it all"*.

I AM TENSE: WHAT CAN I DO ABOUT IT?

There are two phases to any battle. The first is to identify the enemy, to be able to recognise him if you like and the second is to inhibit or to remove him. Our previous section should have covered the first component. The second part is down to you.

It's true to say that *"talk is cheap"*. It is far easier to advise on what to do than actually to do it. Stress is partly a result of character, personality and the part 'ego' plays in your life. If you want to get rid of stress, you may have to make some changes. .

At the end of the debate, you have to make a decision about what is more important to you. If you suffer stress-induced IBS, do you want to go on living with it, or do you want to change something in order to reduce it?

There are really two ways of reducing stress. The first is the passive and mental approach, the second is positive and practical.

PASSIVE AND MENTAL

Can you think without using words? Try it? Do you say to yourself *"I'll get up from this chair and go to make a cup of coffee"*, or do you just do it. We all talk to ourselves to some degree and much self-talk is stressing. This especially happens when you mentally go over again a situation which made you anxious, or you think about a person who is giving you hassle.

Many people are able to develop the trick of instant shut-off and rapid change for the better. As soon as the first few words of a repeated bad scenario come into their mind, they say *"No"* and deliberately switch their thinking to something positive and pleasant. It is a trick, but it can be learned, just as the conscious review described below can be self-taught.

Let your mind fill again with pictures and words from a scene which really upset you – say an argument with your boss, only this time go over it again and make yourself do it differently. You will count up to five before you begin every riposte. You will breathe slowly and deeply and consciously let your shoulders sag and your hands unclench. You will run over the scene a dozen times and each time your performance in it will be more to your advantage. You will be less tense and calmer and more positive in your arguments.

Next time you are in a similar scene, what you have already rehearsed will work for you. It will enable you to relax a little and you will certainly remember some of the clever and positive things you said in your repeated dream scenario and will be able to use them for real. To be prepared is the best way to win.

A personal friend and IBS sufferer who used to get very up-tight with his prickly work colleagues – superior and lower level – relates the following story.

"About three years ago, I went through a very bad patch. My job is not easy and there are frequent minor confrontations and differences of opinion. With hindsight, they were mostly totally unnecessary and many of them occurred only because we had some unpleasant people in the company. The managing director and I were almost permanently at loggerheads. He was a weak-willed bully, suspicious of everybody's motives and forever playing one person off against another behind their backs.

"These regular, vicious arguments would not leave me alone. I began to think about the ones to come as soon as I woke up in the morning and brooded about those which had happened when I got home in the evening. Most bad work scenes are caused by people rather than the job itself.

"I developed this trick of imagining my boss totally nude and caught sexually in flagrante delicto with his unpleasant wife. I used to imagine them at it in all sorts of off-beat places. The spectacle was so ridiculous that the man was totally unable to dominate me from then on. As soon as he started to give me grief, this mental picture came back and I calmed down into internal laughter.

"Then one day I had the trade union convenor banging on my desk about something trivial, so I did the same sexual act trick with him. I actually grinned when he was in mid harangue, so he stopped short. I suggested that he go away and think about it, then come back to see me again when I was in a mood to take it more seriously. Do you know, he never did."

These are some of the passive things which you can do to lessen the number of occasions you get up-tight and to lessen the tension to which you wind up your own stress spring. If you can dominate stress, it is absolutely certain that you will also begin to win your battle against the unpleasantnesses which IBS brings.

POSITIVE AND PRACTICAL

If stress-occasioned IBS develops because of the way you live your life, then changing some parts of your life will reduce the IBS problem. That is logical and unarguable, so solving the problem is really down to you. What minor changes can you make to reduce the stress in your life?

For a start you can look at that list of stress symptoms, work out what causes them at home, at work and in your social life and get rid of some of the less important ones.

- You could have a house rule that you and your wife will both sit down with a glass of wine before dinner every evening.
- You can have a couple of evenings where you do not take work home, but watch television instead.
- You could sit down to breakfast instead of eating it as you dress.
- You could drive to work by a different route and have some days when your car telephone is off the hook.

Instead of being the busy, dynamic, go-getter person you are now, deliberately put off appointments and slow down decisions so that people say of you *"Bill is a very smooth, laid-back sort of guy."* The laid-back brigade rarely suffer IBS. However, if you still think that stress is inevitable, here are a couple of other instances which should convince you otherwise.

SOME MODELS TO FOLLOW

One of the most dynamic and successful business people I know, makes himself sit in an armchair with his eyes closed for thirty minutes at the end of every lunch break. He does not sleep, but makes a conscious effort to empty his brain. He tries to think of nothing. If worrying thoughts or niggles creep in, he switches his thinking and imagining to something different and pleasant. This knack takes a bit of time to acquire, but the more often you try it the easier it becomes.

This siesta is such an invariable and inviolable part of Dan's life that he takes no calls and brooks no interruptions for thirty minutes. This has slowed him down and he gets some of his best ideas during, or just after, this. Above all, he has reduced his stress potential and has improved his digestion so that mouth acidity and rumbling tummy are very rare things.

At one time my partner and I used to spend eleven months a year in the office. The rhythm changed when we bought a cruising yacht and went off for five months. During this period we worked, but I also fretted about letters piling up, a jam of faxes clogging the machine, unpaid bills and clients thinking that we had deserted them. It was relatively pointless worry.

When we returned in September, it took but a morning to sort the post and get the telephone reconnected, so I need not have worried about them whilst I was away. When I rang my best clients to announce my return, they were all pleased to get the call, but none of them had really missed us.

None of us is ever as important as we like to think we are. These days I do as much as I can before we depart for our Summer travels and we manage a fair amount of work on board the boat, but what does not get done does not get done. What it means is that I can really work like a demon when I get back.

This 'sod the lot of them' attitude to petty officials etc has made me more relaxed and has been beneficial to my bowel. The reduced stress has made us both more efficient and more pleasant beings.

8 Food Intolerance

No ordinary person's guide to irritable bowel syndrome would be complete without a separate section on food intolerance – to use the fashionable term. Unfortunately the 'in' phrase is not really wide enough in its meaning. In addition to food, we ingest drink, medicines, tooth paste and even some substances through our nose and skin.

To be really accurate we should call this part of the irritation 'Selected Substance Intolerance', which is a bit clumsy, so let us stick with what is usual, but be aware of its inaccuracy.

Food intolerance is easy to recognise in its simplest form. It means that certain substances 'do not agree' with you and can cause flatulence, stomach rumbling, diarrhoea, vomiting, bad breath or any combination of these. Almost everybody recognises this very elementary form of stomach problem and most of us have a shortlist of foods and drinks which we know will cause us some form of problem.

My own current bêtes noires are uncooked onion and garlic. I can cope with both when – say – spring onion is used as a decoration rather than a main ingredient and garlic is used in many of my favourite recipes. However, a large quantity of raw onion in a salad, a feast of pickled onions, or massively impregnated garlic bread, all cause me real problems from bad breath to flatulence and rumbling tummy. These foods also seem to take longer to pass through my digestion – but that would be logical if the system is struggling to break them down for absorption.

We all have foods guaranteed to 'repeat' on us, which is the same as having a temporary patch of one of the IBS symptoms. However, a food which 'repeats' today might be perfect tomorrow – or next year. Thus, because your body could cope with eggs in your youth, it does not automatically follow that the same will apply when you are forty. We all change with age and what we are able to eat and drink without discomfort often changes with us.

A NEW PHENOMENON?

There is a school of thought which puts about the idea that food intolerance is a new phenomenon. They argue that as it was not known in the eighteenth century, it must be due to our vastly changed eating habits. This is not correct. It might not have been as well observed and reported but, a browse through literature will reveal that eating things which do not agree and so cause stomach ache, heartburn and flatulence is by no means new. Even Chaucer had it. Food intolerance-induced IBS is typical of the ailment in that it is without one solitary causative factor. Changing your food might remove some of the bad effects, but it might not cure them all.

INTOLERANCE OR ALLERGY?

Amongst medical professionals, one of the most annoying statements must be *"Doctor, I am allergic to lemons"* – or some other food. There is a difference between an inability to digest properly and an allergy.

The dictionary defines an allergy as 'hypersensitivity to a substance that causes the body to react to any contact with that substance'. This, however, falls short of the full truth.

If you have an allergy your body produces allergens to the culprit substances. These allergens react with the culprits to produce the symptoms. In the case of an allergy to pollen (hay fever) it is runny nose and weepy eyes. In food allergies, the allergens combine with the insurgents to produce antibodies which activate cells normally dormant. The histamine group of chemicals which stimulate gastric secretions and dilate blood vessels are typical here.

In some respects, having an allergy produces the same discomforts as IBS, but the range is much narrower and the cause generally traceable (to the allergy). There are specific tests for allergies and sure cures. An allergy is a single known attacker, whereas IBS is like an army of secret agents.

THE FOOD GANGS

Actually isolating one food product which always upsets the bowel is a very difficult thing to do, largely because every person's digestive system is slightly different, so we all have marginally different reactions to the same substances. 'One man's meat is another man's poison' is a very sweeping statement but it has arisen from centuries of observing human reactions.

This same collective observation and experience has identified certain groups of foods against which the body might react unfavourably enough to cause the IBS symptoms to occur with varying degrees of severity. They are:

Cereal related – wheat, corn, barley, oats, groundnut etc.

Dairy products – milk, cheese, yoghurt.

Fatty substances – some meats, fried chips.

Acidic juices – citrus, orange.

Miscellaneous – yeast, alcohol, onions, tobacco smoke.

WHEAT is a very common cause of bowel irritation. It contains a substance called gluten (a mix of glutelin and gliadin) which many people find totally indigestible. The problem is that a vast number of prepared foods contain some form of wheat, so it is very difficult to remove from a standard food regime.

Health shops carry a range of products which are described as being 'wheat free'. If you feel that wheat might be your problem, ask your doctor's advice about trying them. If this does not conflict with any other cure he is prescribing, you will certainly do yourself no harm. Corn, barley etc are not exactly the same as wheat, but they can affect some people in similar fashion.

DAIRY PRODUCTS all derive from milk, which contains a white crystalline form of sugar called lactose, which the bowel breaks down into nutrients by combining it with a specially secreted, single function enzyme (lactase). Obviously, a lactase insufficiency will cause problems. It often happens that a person suffering mild diarrhoea, brought on by any of several things, does not produce enough lactase.

This deficiency also helps to cause diarrhoea, so the cumulative effect makes the patient suffer even more. This is, of course, very typical of IBS. There is no single cause, no easy means of diagnosis and no one universal cure.

FATS AND FATTY MEAT are prime suspects for some people, especially those who suffer abdominal aches and who suffer pain during defecation.

ACIDIC JUICES in moderate quantities are tolerated by most people but can cause all the IBS symptoms if imbibed in amounts sufficient to swamp the body's working acids.

THE MISCELLANEOUS attackers affect everybody differently. It is a case of try it and see. If onions disagree with you, the remedy is self evident.

THE O.T.T. EFFECT

Gluttony is never more glaring as one of the Seven Deadly Sins than in being a prime possible cause of the entire IBS spectrum. Most people can cope with most substances most of the time, but as soon as the amount you eat goes over the top of what feels comfortable whilst you are still at the table, the more likely you are to experience bloating (obvious) and later flatulence and toilet problems.

The more often you overeat, the more the body is unable to cope. This is a very sure path to turning an after-dinner bout of tummy rumble or constipation into a more permanent state of bad health.

DIETS GOOD AND BAD

We shall discuss the so-called 'exclusion diets' more fully in the next chapter but here – en passant – they should just be mentioned.

If IBS is caused by your reaction to one member of a group of irritants, you can only isolate the culprit by a patient process of trial and error. Each trial of cutting out one food must be given enough time for the bowel to be completely emptied of it.

You must also ensure that your exclusion is accurate. In the case of wheat and dairy products, for example, you could be in for a shock if you became an avid reader of the contents labels of the tins and boxes in your local supermarket. Most of them list these substances or their derivatives.

IS IT IN THE MIND?

Even the food intolerance/IBS link cannot escape the interaction of our mental functions and the physical process of changing what we eat into beneficial nutrients and waste products. There have been numerous experiments done on these psychosomatic phenomena both in causing IBS and in making our digestive tract reject certain food.

'Psychosomatic' derives from two Greek words meaning 'mind' and 'body' respectively. Crudely put, a psychosomatic illness is one where a firm belief that you have something wrong with you leads you to (think that you) feel all the symptoms. In some instances you worry so much about getting an ulcer that it develops.

In the case of food intolerance, a person who feels that his diarrhoea is caused by eating bananas may suffer an attack if he thinks that a dish contains this fruit, even though not a scrap of banana has been used in the recipe.

Conversely, there are many recorded cases of banana diarrhoea sufferers being fed a diet with a high (but highly disguised) banana content and because they were not told what they were eating suffered no ill effects whatsoever.

BACK TO THE DOCTOR

This is why there is no substitute for professional help. Tell your doctor what you think and what you plan to try, but listen to his advice. The annoying thing about experts is that they are mostly right.

In this case, you can help your doctor to make a correct diagnosis by giving him a list of the things which lead you to believe that your constipation etc is due to your inability to tolerate certain foods. You do not feel right when you eat them and experience:

- Belching.
- Headache – especially the next day.
- Perspiration – in the two hours following eating.
- Bloating – the feeling that the meal is not 'moving on'.

These are the hallmarks of your digestive system complaining about what you are asking it to turn into useful nutrients. If it complains very often you need some investigation and change.

9   Self-Help With Food

If I had to give this chapter a subsidiary title, I should call it 'The Application of Common Sense'. It's worth stressing that nobody dies of irritable bowel and the symptoms are more often minor and a social inconvenience than they are a serious medical condition. It also bears reiteration that if your constipation, diarrhoea, stomach pain or flatulence are very fierce, or you have had them for several uninterrupted months, you need the help of a doctor and you need it soon. However, if your symptoms are mild and only occur from time to time, there is plenty that you can do to help yourself.

The first approach must be to take a good, long, honest look at yourself, at what you eat and drink, together with how you generally live your life. Most mild IBS self-examinees come to the conclusion, *"I'm a mess."* By this they mean that even though they are very well aware of the general rules for sensible eating, drinking, taking exercise and switching off, something stops them from obeying these rules. If you suffer frequent rumbling tummy and flatulence, have a good look at yourself. Be honest.

How much beer, wine and spirits are you drinking these days? Some alcohol is reputedly beneficial as a relaxer and because it is enjoyable. But are you overdoing it? Think about all that malt, yeast, hops and acid that you are pouring into yourself. Do you really think it is doing your stomach any good? Now imagine all that fermenting liquid swirling around in your stomach and being mixed up with bacon and eggs, the morning doughnut, the midday beef burger or a fatty pork sandwich, the afternoon chocolate biscuit, the Mars bar you gulped down on your way to the station, chicken skin from the evening meal, the pudding, the cheese and biscuits, then a bar of chocolate with your evening beer. You have all that lot mixed together.

If your meals contain a high proportion of baked beans, eggs, pizzas, chips, pasties, sausages and pork pies, the mixture is even more sordid.

On their own, most of these foods and drinks are good. In moderation, they all contain beneficial, health-promoting substances. But the third whisky? That Mars bar? Are you really surprised that your bowels are protesting? If you treat your stomach like a human trash can are you surprised that it creates unpleasant noises and smells? Just picture all that junk swirling around and being attacked by enzymes and acids.

Okay. If mild gluttony is making you feel a mess and your stomach is telling you that you are a bit of a slob really, it is not going to be too traumatic to put it right. Nobody is telling you to stop eating, or even to suffer the misery of any strict diet. It just makes sense to watch what you eat. If bad food is one of the causes of your IBS – it may be the sole cause – then better food can only bring about an improvement.

THE FIRST STEP TO COMMON SENSE

You could start today by cutting the excess. A sensible tea and toast breakfast and a very light lunch, which includes an apple. Cut your wine consumption to two glasses and drink mineral water to top up. One glass of spirits is enough. Opt for a dessert, or cheese and biscuits, but not both. You can then afford to relax the rules a bit at the weekend.

A BIT OF EXERCISE, TOO

Food needs exercise to help it move along. This does not imply that you go to a gymnasium, or join an aerobics class, but it does mean that you would benefit by any regular body movement which makes your pulse go faster and your breathing rate go up.

Beware of jogging. There is a very strong school of medical thought which believes that the human knee joint is one of the worst pieces of engineering design ever created. It can be considerably damaged by an overweight, inexperienced and inexpert runner constantly pounding it onto pavements.

You could, however, walk home from work at a good fast rate. Time yourself and enjoy watching your performance improve. You could even come home by two or three different routes and have a time plan for each of them.

It is a safe bet that just by following the first common sense steps about watching what you eat and being a bit wiser about exercise, you will lose a bit of weight and feel a lot better in yourself. You will also find a noticeable improvement in the way your bowels are behaving.

THE DETOXIFICATION WEEK

A 'detox' week is something which we have done in our own household a number of times. I am able to recommend its benefits from personal experience. It is also good fun and very satisfying to do. It might take a very strong character to be able to do this, but several people doing it together will prop each other up and make it generally more enjoyable.

A detoxification week means that you drink no alcohol and eat no dairy products. (Milk in tea etc is allowed.) You ration yourself to two cups of coffee a day and cut out chocolate. Breakfast is toast and marmalade (white bread or brown), lunch is an apple and a stroll and the evening meals are varieties of fish, chicken and non-fried vegetables. Part of the fun is in devising the menus.

If you wish to add some exercise of a slightly more serious and beneficial nature to the detox week, swimming comes high on the list. It is a good excuse to drag yourself out of the office at lunchtime, or to chase the worries away at the end of the day and before you relax for the evening.

An interesting way to monitor your progress is to 'Target Swim'. Your aim is to count how many lengths you can swim in fifteen minutes – no longer. If you need to rest after every length at first it does not matter. When you can swim your target in, say, twelve minutes, add another length.

In the detox week, you are doing three things: You are giving your bowel manageable foods. You are not asking it to deal with vast quantities. You are exercising enough to help the foods move along the tubes. You will also be feeling one hell of a sight better because you know that you are doing something positive about your health.

WHAT ABOUT FIBRE?

The place and function of fibre in the control of irritable bowel and similar maladies has been – and still is – a matter for continued debate and research. There have been times when medical opinion has been a bit lukewarm about its effectiveness and other periods when doctors have been very enthusiastic about its use.

This is one of the problems of IBS. Nothing is crystal clear, so a high degree of self-help is possible and the use of a high-fibre diet is certain to be beneficial. This is not just book advice, because no matter which way the popularity pendulum has swung, there has never been a time when medical opinion has said that a diet with plenty of roughage is a bad thing. It is not a question of whether fibre is a good IBS controller or not, but of the degree of its effectiveness.

There have also been a large number of hospital patient studies done by putting one group of IBS sufferers on a high-fibre diet and checking their progress against patients not similarly fed. Unfortunately, the results have never thrown up a total one hundred per cent conclusion.

On the other hand, there have been plenty of success stories of cures and improvements brought about by increasing the fibre content of a sufferer's food. The cynics might argue that such relief is largely brought about by the so-called placebo effect – ie you think that something is doing you good, so you begin to get better. This is the down-side, but on the up-side, the realists will be pleased that this does not matter just as long as the patient improves. If you suffer IBS badly enough to seek a cure, the end is much more important than the means.

WHAT DOES FIBRE DO?

Why a high fibre content in food relieves IBS symptoms is not absolutely certain. Its use has arisen more from observation and long experience than from any evidence presented by medical research. There is also some confusion caused in the layman's mind because both constipation and diarrhoea are relieved by the same means.

As already mentioned, some protagonists of the fibre route to cure, see it as the coarser material rubbing against the bowel wall like sandpaper and so simultaneously scrubbing it clean and stimulating the muscles and the enzyme-releasing glands to do their job more effectively.

A second group of experts counsels fibre because there is evidence that some of the substances contained in fibrous vegetables and cereals act as catalysts to make the chemical changes involved in digestion happen more certainly, more thoroughly and at a faster rate.

It is very probable that both schools of thought are correct and that fibre does all these things. Anyway, in spite of the confusing theories, there is plenty of practical experience to indicate that an increase in your dietary fibre will very rarely do any harm and has a very high probability of easing some of the unpleasant, irritating symptoms of IBS.

WHAT SORT OF FIBRE?

Bran is the most often recommended fibre and is contained in a number of breakfast cereals. It can also be taken raw in the forms sold by health food shops and pharmacists. Some people find that this upsets them, so they need to find a less 'coarse' way of ingestion and almost everybody experiences a bit more flatulence over the first few days of taking bran.

In summary, it is worth trying a spoonful a day for a week and if you feel that your bowel is coping, increase this to three times a day with meals. Then the bran will be absorbed with other food and will possibly be more easily digested.

Bran is by no means a modern body cleanser. Even Hippocrates, the godfather of medicine, dubbed bran 'the father of medicine'. It occurs in various forms and has various similar cousins in a very wide range of simple foods besides the specialist proprietary compounds sold by health food shops. So you should be able to find bran, or a bran substitute, which you like and which your body tolerates, but which your IBS symptoms will hate sufficiently to be driven into decline.

The bran cure will be worth trying by eating much more of the following:

- Wholemeal bread and granary bread.
- Specialist cereals and mueslis.
- Apples, pears, plums etc including their skins.
- Normal vegetables such as cabbage, swede etc.
- Uncooked vegetables like carrot, celery and lettuce.
- Baked beans, mushy peas, pulses.
- Dried fruit.
- Wholemeal pasta.
- Plenty of beans – including soya, butter and haricot.
- 'Coarser' home-made soup with plenty of diced vegetables.
- A prescribed bulking agent such as Isogel.

THE RESULTS MATTER MOST

If you follow the normal pattern, you will find that your visits to the toilet will become much more comfortable. Your stools will become larger and of a much more median texture – ie neither the hardness of near constipation, nor having the runny consistency of diarrhoea. Your food will also take less time to pass through the system and you will generally feel better all round. The control of IBS is very much a matter of making yourself feel physically and mentally well.

WHERE CAN I FIND A READY-MADE HIGH-FIBRE DIET?

Most of us are not food experts and neither are we very imaginative about devising menus. Happily, there are a number of cookery books dealing with this topic alone and they contain some very appetising high-fibre meals. My own local bookshop has half a dozen books on healthy eating and special diet cookery books. The microfiche catalogue in the local library has an even longer list.

If you are nervous about a DIY fibre increase, your doctor will probably have a number of pre-printed diet sheets available. They will advise something like the following:

MORNING MEAL
Fruit juice, grapefruit or melon, porridge, a bran or whole wheat, crispy cereal, wholemeal bread, oatcakes or wholemeal waffles, chunky marmalade – plenty of peel.
MIDDAY
Vegetable soups, wholemeal bread sandwiches of lettuce etc.
EVENING
Meat, chicken, fish, wholemeal bread, salads, lightly cooked vegetables, greens and beans, jacket potatoes, fruit.

This is not to point you towards the extremes of the 'nut cutlet' exponents, but it will introduce a more wholesome content into your food and leave plenty of room for an appetising variety without resort to fatty, proprietary packets and tins.

THE EXCLUSION DIET

If your minor IBS has not cleared itself up by the means already suggested, it could be because the irritation is being caused by your particular body's reaction to just one substance, or to a group of food constituents.

The only sure way of finding out which group adversely affects you is by cutting out certain foods for a while and monitoring the effects.

This is a cure of much patience and committed attention to detail.

If you do not feel confident about making your own plan of what foodstuffs to leave out and cannot find one in a book, your doctor will almost certainly have one. However, no matter whether you are a DIY excluder, or doctor guided, you will need to keep notes not only about the dates, times and constituents of what you eat or drink, but also to keep a note of the consistency of the stools that you pass.

Your guidelines will probably be a variation of the list below, with each group excluded for a week to ten days at a time.

EXCLUDE	NOTES
TEA	Herbal tea is OK
COFFEE	Even decaffeinated
FRUIT JUICE	Try tomato juice
ALCOHOL	
TAP WATER	Bottled water is OK
COW'S MILK	Try goat's milk
EGGS	
CHEESE	
BUTTER	
VEGETABLE OIL	Cook with sunflower or walnut oil
WHEAT, OATS ETC	Use rice instead
WHITE BREAD	
SHELL/SMOKED FISH	
ONIONS	
ALL PRESERVED MEATS	
CHOCOLATE	

You can exclude these things in related groups.

THE YEAST BEAST

Yeast is a very common cause of wind and diarrhoea. It is also very difficult to exclude completely because it is used in so many different food processes.

Rather than attempt an exclusion isolation, you can take a small quantity of brewer's yeast on a small piece of bread for a couple of days. If this does not cause you markedly increased flatulence, mild diarrhoea or possibly a slightly sore rectum, you do not have a yeast intolerance problem.

Whatever happens, you cannot do yourself any lasting harm and even the bad effects disappear in a day. However, if irritations do occur, or are exacerbated by this minute quantity of yeast, you should see your doctor, who will be able to prescribe a yeast neutralising drug.

FINAL WORDS

All the anti-IBS methods described above will only work well if you give them a chance.

This means:

- Sticking to the plan.
- Eating at regular times.
- Always sitting down to eat.
- Never eat so much that you do not want more.
- Chew your food thoroughly into small pieces.

In addition to dietary self-help, there are plenty of other things you can do to relieve yourself of the irritable bowel inconvenience. As you will see in the next chapter, most of these are positive steps which will even enrich your life in ways over and above the basic aim of providing relief from that irritable bowel.

10 Self-Help – Relax

Relaxation is a physical phenomenon brought about by a state of mind and vice versa. If your muscles are tense because you are in a panic situation or a period of stress, they will not relax until you have your thoughts and emotions under control again. Conversely, if your muscles are working very hard to avoid danger – hanging on for dear life – when they finish the task your brain will also relax.

This might sound a bit familiar, but it is an inescapable fact of physiological engineering that your bowel is controlled by muscles. If they are tense, then this will cause all the minor/major digestive tract problems that IBS means. As we have said before, the problems of an irritable bowel can worry you into getting really up-tight and this in itself exaggerates the bowel irritation. The mental state affects the physical and vice versa so that the problem gets to be like a pendulum whose arc of irritation gets wider and more serious with every oscillation.

YOUR OWN PERSONALITY

There is very little anybody can do to force a major change in personality. In broad terms, we are what we were when we were born. Personality traits are more genetic and inherited than caused by environment and education. So, the best we can hope for is to make minor adjustments to enable you to cope with irritable bowel. How we use personality to combat IBS will obviously vary from person to person, but the example below is illustrative of minor processes to reduce tension, to diminish stress and to get the bowels back to normal. Let us call our subject Bob.

BOB

Bob is the sort of person who finds it absolutely impossible to sit still and do nothing for more than a few minutes at a time. He is not hyperactive and not a prime case to contract IBS, but neither will he escape it altogether. He just has lots of physical and mental energy.

For instance, he enjoys fishing, but is quite unable to wait patiently for a catch. *"I either catch fish immediately or go home."* Neither can Bob lie idle in the sun for long periods, even though he is envious of those who can. On the beach, he throws stones at driftwood, goes for a walk, uses the binoculars when there is nothing to see and generally fidgets. Unless a television programme is good, Bob walks out of the lounge in search of some other diversion.

Should his personality and other circumstances get him onto the IBS rack, it will not go away of its own accord. Luckily, there are a number of things he could do to slow himself down enough to deal with the complaint:

- Read thrillers and adventure stories, which would, in a sense, channel his energy through the fictitious characters in the books.
- Do a Walter Mitty – close his eyes and imagine himself flying a Spitfire or climbing Everest. He can have his adventures with very little physical or mental fatigue.
- Find a hobby which makes him sit still – the attraction of model making or listening to opera.

In summary then, we cannot change our basic personality, but we can all develop better attitudes, be receptive and more accommodating to the habits and desires of those closest to us in order to avoid friction. If your partner likes sunbathing, you could learn to read or play solitaire. In that way, neither of you gets up-tight with the other.

THE CAR AS A STRESS AGENT

The car brings as many perils as it brings pleasures. It is probably responsible for more frustration, anger and stress than any other man-made machine. Tension and higher heart rate are caused by slow moving traffic, other drivers, worry and increased pulse rate when overtaking, apprehension about speeding and being caught by the police, doubts about mechanical efficiency and anxiety about HP payments and maintenance bills.

One antidote to all this tension is to talk to yourself.

- Tell yourself that you are a better driver than the others.
- Enjoy the slower pace of a traffic queue.
- If you are being forced to go slowly there is no chance of a speeding ticket.
- Slow means safe, less wear on the car and less wear and tear on the driver. You may not be crawling by choice, but as you are stuck with it, you may as well appreciate its good side.
- If someone shouts at you and makes rude signs, reflect on how that is harming his bowel. Just grin. His problem does not have to become your problem too.
- Better twenty minutes late for an appointment than twenty years early in heaven – or wherever.

One of the least stressful parts of my own life is the annual five months where we move the office onto the boat and never drive the car. However, I feel my hackles rise in the first traffic jam I meet when we get back.

One thing which helps is to do a commentary on your own driving.

"Nothing in the mirror – pulling into near side to get an early look round this right hander – red car in the mirror – speed sign coming up – brake lights ahead – two cars in the mirror – changing down one for the bend" and so on. This takes your mind off all the things likely to upset you and even calms you down by making you drive a bit better.

TELEPHONE TENSIONS

One of the most successful businessmen I know is a very calm, laid-back character whose telephone is right next to his elbow. When it rings, he deliberately lets it sound a few times as he pulls notepad and pencil into position. Then he gives his number – never his name

– and makes himself count five before he utters his first words.

"It took me a few weeks to force myself into this technique. I did it because I always jumped and felt my heart miss a beat when a call came in. Now the telephone does not irritate me any more and the best compliment was a young lady who said that she always enjoyed calling me because I was never snappy and always polite."

WORK – THE MENTAL TOURNIQUET

We should recognise that our attitude to work is as much governed by personality as by the actual job. Those doctors who advise IBS sufferers to take on less work and to devise a more relaxed schedule, should also be aware of another side of the coin.

There are many people who are very proud of their dynamic working image and who are only relaxed and happy when they have a fast car, a mobile telephone and a busy schedule of meetings. These are all part of their prized image and they feel tense and deprived when they do not have them. They counter the pleas *"Slow down, the plodders also get there"* with the answer that carthorses are extinct.

If you belong to this group, you may have to look elsewhere for your IBS causes. If something is giving you pleasure, it will not be doing any harm – even if it is a round of meetings and telephone calls.

Another side to be considered is the people you work with – there is nothing you can do to change them. Your best hope is to help them to change their attitude to you and the best way to do that is to show total insouciant calm.

Like military tactics, calm comes from good planning. If you know that you are in for a stressful meeting with a boss or a colleague, force yourself to plan the session in advance and to be prepared for the way it might go. If you visualise several different scenarios and possible answers to questions, you will be able to combine possibilities and to adapt your visualisations to make sure that you get your point of view heard.

An excellent tactic is to smile, no matter how you feel and always to count up to five before you speak. (If your stress-maker is fiery, pushy and apoplectic, the more you slow down, the more he will speed up and the more you should try to slow down again. It's his problem.)

It is not a bad idea to arrive a few minutes late, not in a rush, deliberately calm and never apologise. The slow speaking, pausing Prime Minister Winston Churchill was an excellent exponent of the sort of tension reducers we are talking about. This is well illustrated in a snippet from one of his meetings with King George VI.

GRVI *"Mr Prime Minister, why are you late?"*

WC *"I left late, Your Majesty."*

Unanswerable and a super de-tensioner. Here are some other things you can do:

- Always take your full lunch and coffee breaks and take them away from your desk.
- If you need to go to the toilet during work time, do not try to resist. Go and go slowly.

THE STRESSFUL REST PERIOD

There is a super Breton countryman/fisherman proverb which says: *"I need to make myself rest today so that I will do four days work tomorrow."*

If you are unable to enjoy your evenings and weekends, there are certainly a number of things which you can do. You may hate gardening so much that this increases tension. So find some other activity you might enjoy.

The first thing for you and your partner to do is to write out seperate lists of the things you may be able to do together. Write down all your ideas no matter how fanciful, meaningless, impossible, irreverent or irrelevant. Then amalgamate the lists under headings. The final document could look like this:

ACTIVITY	YES	NO	MAYBE
Have a second holiday	Mary		John
Decorate the spare room	Mary/John		
Join a golf club		Mary	John
Play cards tomorrow	Mary/John		

THE HAPPY MEDIUM

In conclusion, we must all seek our own level. If you know that your job is contributing to your irritable bowel, but you like your job, or there is no way you can alter what you do to any great degree, the decision is yours. Only you can decide what sort of compromise you are willing to make to get your flatulence and constipation under control. It is your life. People can advise, but only you can decide what is most important to you.

Even if you are a workaholic, you can certainly find ways to relax a bit. If you can get your tension level down, your irritable bowel seriousness will almost certainly sink with it.

THE ROLE OF RELAXATION

Our subject, Bob is typical of many people who do not know how to relax. It is an acquired skill, more easily learned by some personality groups than by others. You cannot consciously force yourself to relax, but you can deliberately create odd moments when you allow yourself to unwind for a few seconds. Once you have given yourself a chance, you are a few steps towards being one of those very lucky people who can switch off and go into a semi-trance at will.

The way to get on the road is by trying the thirty second total flop-out technique. Everybody can make thirty spare seconds.

Just where you are sitting right now – home, commuter train, office – start to feel tension pouring out of separate parts of your body. Talk to yourself in your mind. Imagine that your neck is feeling relaxed, loose and floppy. Feel that your right shoulder is oiled and that your arm is actually stretching out to be a bit longer. Do not pull in your tummy muscles. Let it all hang out for a moment.

If a part of you does not seem to be responding, ignore it and move to another part. As soon as you manage to induce this feeling of total relaxation into some parts of your body, try to remember the sensation you get as you feel the tension just draining and oozing out of you. It's a very physical sensation.

This memory must then be the starting point for your next thirty second flop-out session. You begin by recalling the feeling, then begin to think that your neck, shoulder etc are achieving the feeling again. Every time you succeed, you improve your chances of further, more comprehensive, deeper relaxation. The length of the period will also increase.

If you could inculcate a two minute total, weightless feeling of relaxation into your work routine three times a day, that would be very good news for your well-being and very bad news for IBS problems. The case is unarguable. Irritable bowel syndrome is partly caused by tension. Relaxation removes tension. Less tension means a less irritated bowel.

SERIOUS RELAXATION

Once you accept the argument, you will also see a good case for a regular period of very serious relaxation. Here we are talking about twenty minutes or so per day, either as one session or split up. It is, however, a very short period of time.

A number of readers will now be saying *"Where do you expect me to find a place on my own and the time to take a regular twenty minutes off each day?"*

If you have thought about asking those questions and are an IBS sufferer, you are one hundred per cent the sort of person who needs deliberate relaxation.

HOW TO RELAX

Where you try to relax does not really matter. It is more a state of mind than a physical act. However, the state of mind is more easily achieved if you are somewhere warm, quiet and comfortable. A sofa is probably best, so that you can lie on your back with your body in a shallow U shape – like a saucer – with your head supported on a cushion and your feet on a slightly higher level. Your shoes should be off and your clothing loose. Put your arms where they feel most comfortable. Close your eyes.

You can also relax on an upright chair with a cushion beneath your buttocks and another in the small of your back. It is essential that you get your feet flat on the floor, or on a raised surface. Let your spine be upright and your shoulders touch the chair back if it is high enough. Your head comes gently forward, chin on chest, and your arms rest palms down on your thighs.

Once in position, make a conscious effort to empty your mind. Free it of words. Only you know what your problems and irritants are. If one of them crops up in your mind, drive it away. Give it the antidote treatment of deliberately and immediately thinking about something pleasant.

Do not expect to reach a totally relaxed state at the first attempt, but you can be confident that every try will bring it closer and will push some of the IBS poisons further away.

WHEN TO RELAX

The period of the day to switch off is yours to decide. One man I know does it on the train and another uses five minutes of his coffee and tea breaks and ten minutes during his lunch hour. There are people who practise relaxation just after they get up and just before they go to bed. These would be my worst times. Before the evening meal, in the bath, before dinner – these are good times. A bad time to pick is just after a meal. Your metabolism and other systems are a bit busy just then, so keep them awake and at it.

VERY SERIOUS RELAXATION

Here is not the place to advise people who wish to take this a stage further. This is a book about the relief of IBS and relaxation obviously has its place in the text. Yoga, spiritualism and meditation could all be good curative agencies for those who have the time and the talent to indulge and the will to go further along this path.

There are plenty of books on relaxation techniques and exercises for the really committed. Classes for more esoteric but comprehensive mental and physical calm are everywhere. So if you are serious, there is plenty of help available.

BIOFEEDBACK TECHNIQUES

If you like gadgets and are a fan of modern electronics, the biofeedback route to relaxation is a very interesting voyage. It works on the principle that the higher your level of tension the greater the number of electrical messages passing through your body. There are a number of surface 'pressure points' where this signal level can be monitored.

Therefore, when you move from stress and tension into beneficial relaxation, the electrical activity diminishes.

Engineers have designed measuring machines using simple electrodes which are stuck onto named body points with tape. The head, the chest, even the ends of your fingers are all possibilities.

The degree of electrical/muscular activity can be shown as a light-emitting diode which gets brighter as you get tense, or as your pulse rate increases. A pointer can be used, or even a metronome which matches your state by speeding and slowing.

Some people need to go to biofeedback classes to learn both the machine and how to become less tense. They are run in many private hospitals and alternative medicine clinics and the NHS has an increasing body of practitioners. You could ask your doctor about the possibilities.

An alternative would be to buy your own machine. They are relatively inexpensive and regularly advertised. The aim is to teach yourself to watch the indicator and to observe what thoughts/movements/ideas cause the monitor to increase and vice versa. When you provoke zero response, you are totally relaxed.

FINAL WORDS

It is extremely unlikely that biofeedback or any of the other self-help, relaxation and anti-IBS techniques discussed in this chapter would interfere with any treatment your doctor is offering. If in doubt, consult him. Tell him what you plan and he might offer even more help.

We must never forget that irritable bowel syndrome is a complaint which is largely self-induced and that the cure will most often be in your own hands and mind. If you want to rid yourself of it, you can and will.

11 Extra Sources Of Help

In researching this book, there have been very many times when we have been saddened by stories of how long-term IBS sufferers have had their lives upset by irritable bowels. Surprisingly perhaps, there have been almost as many moments when we have felt very sorry for the doctors.

As we have pointed out a number of times, the root-causes of IBS are often so complex and so obscure that the doctor has to try many things to locate them. He generally appreciates that the patient is becoming more and more depressed and that the symptoms are not getting less. Whilst the poor doctor desperately wants to effect a cure and really wants to help the patient back to happiness and normality, they both need a bit of luck in their search.

This relatively common failure to find fast relief does not imply any lack of knowledge or competence on the part of the doctor, nor any lack of co-operation by the patient. It is more a testimony to the complicated and baffling aspects of IBS and the interactions between the patient's mind and his body. At about this point, many IBS sufferers will start to get something of a loss of confidence in conventional medicine and its treatments and begin to think of other sources of help.

Alternative Medicine is something of a Harlequin – a trade of many colours, sometimes touched with comedy and occasionally having the charlatan's reputation for deception. But at other times, treatment which is on the fringe of the healing scene had some very spectacular curative successes.

There are certainly plenty of case studies in which treatment of IBS by people who are not qualified doctors has worked well. It should also be realised that a number of doctors of medicine are also qualified homoeopaths and have expertise in other fringe methods of treatment. These are variously dubbed Alternative Medicine, Complementary Medicine and Holistic Medicine

ALTERNATIVE MEDICINE?

The whole area of treatment by non-conventional means has become confused by its own diffusion and esoteric titles. Grandfather would probably have consulted a village elder who was known to be an expert at 'home' cures. Unfortunately, life is no longer this simple because there are so many forms of alternative medicine and they all have different names. The potential patient needs to approach this area with a little care and in the knowledge that not all the treatment methods are suitable for all types of people and only some forms of alternative medicine are suitable as an IBS cure. To enable you to choose your extra/alternative consultant, the normal divisions are as follows:

ACUPUNCTURE is a treatment whereby the tips of very fine needles are inserted into the skin at various places believed to stimulate certain nerves, which in turn act to cure specific disorders. The system is very old and practised in so many parts of the world that it has to be seen as more than just a theory.

A typical first acupuncture consultation will be about an hour of questions and answers. The specialist is looking for leads to the root cause of IBS and making sure of a correct diagnosis. Acupuncturists work by three methods:

- They hope to treat the cause and by removing it also to let the symptoms clear up in the process.
- They recognise that thoughts and emotions cause illnesses and that certain parts of the body have a connection with emotion eg tickling the feet makes people happy enough to laugh.
- They know that all organs have sympathetic nerves which control their proper function and where these nerves are close to the surface they can be stimulated (by needles) so that they work properly.

This first session will certainly recommend a change of diet – generally to a much simpler regime – in order to create a good foundation for the second consultation. At this, up to half a dozen needles might be inserted at nerve points which are connected to the bowel and which affect the muscle action and secretions of the colon. These points are generally located in the feet, forearm and lower back and because none of them is near a vein, there will be no bleeding.

The needles are very fine. They are only about the thickness of a hair so the patient rarely feels their insertion and there is no discomfort during the quarter of an hour whilst they are in place.

A normal course of treatment might be once a week for a month and does have a good track record in the treatment of 'nerve-related' complaints. Most patients say that the treatment has made them feel *"generally more healthy"*. Once you can say that, you are already on the road to conquering IBS by following the absolutely true dictum that, 'Positive health is a marvellous healer'.

Be sure to choose a properly qualified and registered acupuncturist. If you have any doubts about an individual, you can check with the regulating and registration body whose address is listed in the appendix.

AROMATHERAPY probably dates from ancient Egypt, but has been enjoying a recent boom initiated in France and spreading outwards. As the name implies, the therapy devolves from massaging aromatic oils into the skin.

Reputation has it that some oils used on the exterior have a direct effect on certain interior functions. More realistic practitioners seem to favour the view that firstly the subject must genuinely like the smell of the oil being used. Secondly, that the most therapeutic value comes from inducing a feeling of well-being allied to total relaxation. It is the relaxation of a good massage but with increased benefits from the special lubricants.

There are just a few NHS hospitals with nurses trained in the selection of oils and the massage techniques. Some alternative medicine group centres have a specialist, but most are private practitioners.

The best of these will belong to the professional association whose address we quote later. Aromatherapy also has a strong tradition of self-massage.

CHIROPRACTIC is a method of treating bodily malfunctions by manipulation of the spine. The theory is that because the spine carries the main cord of the nervous system, if it gets out of alignment or suffers other deformation, the nerves and the nervous control of muscles and other functions will all suffer.

We have no personal or other direct knowledge of chiropractic cure or relief of IBS symptoms, but the national association may have some case histories.

HERBALISM is as old as Man. The basic principle is that certain herbs, either rubbed on externally as an ointment, or taken internally as powders and potions, produce specific effects. A vast number of these effects concern the treatment of common illnesses.

The logic of this is indisputable. If you believe that drugs can cure and if you know that the substances they contain are usually derived from plants and other natural sources, you must agree that herbs should have similar properties. In herbalism, many ailments are treated with camomile, aniseed, valerian, arrowroot, peppermint, betony, marshmallow, lavender and so on – either solo or in compounds.

It is essential that the IBS sufferer seeking this route to relief should consult a properly qualified and registered herbalist. Some herbal substances can be dangerous in certain conditions – pregnancy for instance – so you should also let your doctor know what you intend.

Some medical practices can recommend a herbalist and the professional institute will also advise. Ideally, they should have case histories of the use of herbal medicine in bowel disorder treatment.

HOMOEOPATHY is the science of treating illness by using very small amounts of the sort of drug which would cause a healthy person to show symptoms of the malady in question. It is a system of treating like with like, or the theory of the counter irritant. Homoeopathy is very similar to vaccination ie you inject a minute amount of – say – flu germ into the body to help it fight flu.

Explained in another way, the homoeopath believes that symptoms of an illness are partly the sign that the human body is itself producing the antidote to fight it. Thus you give it a bit of help with a bit more antidote.

A course of homoeopathic treatment will – as always – begin with diagnostic questioning to establish the real nature of the complaint. The healer will then prescribe a cure, which is very often in the form of tablets. He will point out that these are 'pure' substances which must be stored in sterile conditions and taken under strict guidelines.

The medicines will differ according to the symptoms but we would not recommend a 'do-it-yourself' approach by purchasing general homoeopathy pills from a pharmacist. It is much better to consult a practitioner with qualifications and who is registered with one of the national organisations.

There are many doctors who are also qualified homoeopaths. In the case of IBS, their detractors say that they are treating the symptoms – eg diarrhoea – rather than the root-causes. However, the practice has a good reputation against IBS and it must be agreed that diminishing the symptoms will reduce tension and anxiety and this will have a further good influence towards a total cure.

HYPNOTHERAPY is really an extension and intensification of the relaxation techniques which we discussed in chapter ten. Treatment consists of putting the patient into a shallow form of hypnosis. This bears absolutely no relation to the hypnotic state brought about – or pretended – by stage performers. The sleep technique is totally aimed at getting the patient to relax, which – as we know – is very, very beneficial in the anti-IBS fight.

One of the principal advantages of treating IBS by hypnotherapy is that the totally relaxed patient is more ready to talk uninhibitedly about personal matters and personal habits. This can help with a more accurate recognition of the real root-cause – the source of the worry, or the real reason for the tension which is having such a bad effect on the bowel.

A well conducted hypnotherapy session is usually a very enjoyable experience. It is not harmful and does not have any bad side-effects. Indeed, quite the opposite occurs because a person coming out of medical hypnosis normally experiences a feeling of relaxed well-being. This can only do good.

A good hypnotherapist will teach the patient to induce a state of semi-trance in himself. This is just one teeny step further than the total relaxation techniques we talked about in the previous chapter.

A number of doctors practice hypnotic cures and many patients feel more comfortable with a hypnotherapist who is also a fully qualified doctor. It should also be said, however, that hypnotherapy is quite harmless and depends on total patient co-operation. If you do not wish to be put into a semi-trance, or if you decide to resist once the process has started, there is absolutely no way that you can be forced to 'go under'. Once you are in the hypnotic state, neither is there any danger that you might be forced into doing anything which you find distasteful.

The British Hypnotherapy Association, whose address is listed at the back of the book, will certainly assure you on this point and will be able to recommend a qualified therapist.

OSTEOPATHY is a system of healing by manipulating bones and other parts of the body. The science is, in fact, both broader and deeper than this dictionary-style definition and is possibly the most senior branch of what is loosely called 'holistic' medicine, a treatment system which sees the body as a complete entity. If one part is out of alignment, there is a knock-on effect causing other structures not to be in their proper place.

In the case of IBS, the osteopath will look for anything which might cause parts of the digestive tract to be put under strain so that the muscles and membranes supporting it are stretched. He might also be looking for parts which should not be touching and which might therefore be receiving wrong messages and stimuli. This, in turn, causes them to secrete incorrect amounts of enzymes, or to have irregular muscular contractions.

Irritable bowel is often a matter of the automatic muscles not working properly – eg too slowly. An osteopath will massage and palpate to give them improved reflexes and to start them going again. Most osteopaths are also well versed in balanced diets.

However, the warning bears repeating. Search out an osteopath who is qualified and registered with the General Council and Register of Osteopaths (see Useful Addresses).

REFLEXOLOGY bears a certain similarity to acupuncture, but works on a much less complex level and does not involve needles. The reflexologist massages parts of the soles of the feet in a manner which is said to promote and stimulate blood supply and to calm the nerves. The link between this therapy and IBS is enhanced because part of the arch of the foot, back toward the heel, has an internal structure which looks like a bowel. Many practitioners believe that there is a very strong sympathetic connection between the big tract in the stomach and its miniature version in the foot.

Reflexology is quite suitable for self-treatment. You sit upright so that you can put your foot in your lap, then massage the area mentioned above by moving your finger tips along the foot in a toes-to-heel direction. The sensation is very soothing and relaxing and can only be beneficial.

WHAT IS BEST?

The observant will have noticed that I have discussed the various branches of alternative and complementary medicine in strictly alpha-betical order. The introductions above are in no sense a league table nor an order-of-merit list.

Neither did I have any strong personal feeling for or against some of the claims made by the healers. There is no place for the war which some doctors seem to have declared on alternative medicine and these critics always ignore the fact that some of their own equally well-qualified and experienced colleagues (some very eminent) are also practitioners of alternative cures. Many private clinics and NHS hospitals employ this sort of specialist.

The point here is that IBS is such a complicated and highly individual state of affairs that anything which does you no harm, but which could well do you much good, is worth trying.

As the mind and body are so complex, they should be seen as a total entity with one part depending on the other. The medical profession has perhaps become prone to too much separation and specialisation. The ENT (ear, nose, throat) specialist and the heart disease consultant are excellent at diagnosing specific ailments. It could well be that in curing some of them they cause spin-off effects in other parts of the body.

This is certainly true of some healing drugs and the contraceptive pill is another good example of a drug designed for one specific effect in one area, creating other effects in a different body part or system.

The idea of total medicine to cure ailments is a very attractive proposition in IBS treatment. The main thing which has come out of our research is the totality of the complaint. It affects mind and body and could well respond to a total personal cure. The practitioner of alternative medicine will involve the patient in the cure and during the course of treatment will also try to make the whole person well.

12 The End Of The Beginning

Books are like wheels in the way they come full circle back to their starting point. Their value is in what you get out of them along the way and the author, in its preparation and research, derives as much learning and help as the reader.

Certainly all my research has reinforced my initial impressions that Irritable Bowel Syndrome is a medical problem which has not yet been tackled with the enthusiasm and big guns brought to bear on such complaints as influenza. It remains a medical puzzle looking for someone to find the solution.

But that is partly the nature of a syndrome. It is a bit like an octopus with tentacles everywhere. Quite often you feel that if you surgically remove one of them, it will grow again elsewhere. The fear is that any form of treatment might cure one of the symptoms, but might exacerbate others or even create a new malady.

There is also the much-discussed action and interaction between physical and psychological aspects of IBS. Many of the problems are brought on by ourselves. This, of course, is also a ray of remedial light.

If something within us brings about the unpleasant symptoms and if the things we do in our daily lives bring on IBS, then it logically follows that we have it in us to do something about it. No matter whether the problem is created by stress, by food, or by some physical factor, the sufferer can himself do much to assist the cure.

If your symptoms are only mild, have a go at getting rid of them by relaxation and detoxification. If the symptoms are severe or persistent go to see your doctor, but go in a positive frame of mind. If you feel that he has not considered IBS as a possibility, tell him what you have read and what you think. If your doctor does not agree then ask him to recommend a second opinion.

Whilst you must have the patience to continue the prescribed treatment, you should be able to report progress towards positive health within a month. If this does not happen, go back to the doctor and ask for a review of the prescription, or with a plea to try something different.

Neither should you be totally diverted from any self-help plans you have and these could well include trying cures on the periphery of mainstream medicine. As previously discussed, several branches of so-called alternative medicine have a proven record of assistance and relief to IBS sufferers.

It may well be that your doctor knows where this sort of help can be obtained within the National Health Service, or financed by your private (or company) health insurance. If this is impossible, be frank with your doctor by telling him that you intend to find your own alternative unless he advises you of any dangers of such treatment.

Also be comforted by the fact that you are not alone in your suffering. There really are millions of others just like you. These numbers have been allowed to grow because the research has been insufficient and this lack is permitted because IBS is neither fatal nor contagious.

This picture is beginning to change. Even this book is part of the recognition that IBS exists as a widespread malady. There is now an organised body offering comfort and practical advice in the form of a newsletter. It can be obtained from:

IBS Network, c/o The Centre for Human Nutrition, Northern General Hospital, Herries Road, Sheffield S5 7AU.

The newsletter is called *Gut Reaction*. If you would like a sample copy and to know more about the Network, be sure to include an adequately sized stamped addressed envelope.

So the help is all around you and within you but it will not work of its own accord. The relief of IBS must be triggered off by yourself.

You have taken the first step by reading these words. That is the end of the beginning of your cure. Now it is up to you!

Glossary

ACETYLCHOLINE	the chemical which triggers off muscle contraction when released at the nerve endings
ADRENALINE	a hormone which puts all the body's faculties on top line. A creator of energy and preparation for action
ALLERGY	a reaction to contact with certain substances which creates adverse effects on body functions
ANTIBIOTIC	a substance such as penicillin produced by body micro-organisms and capable of inhibiting or destroying other organisms – especially bacteria
ANTISPASMODIC	slowing down or stopping spasms eg an antispasmodic drug
ANUS	the opening through which the body discharges solid waste products
ANXIOLYTIC	a low power tranquilliser often prescribed by doctors
AUTONOMIC NERVOUS SYSTEM	that part of the body which controls such involuntary actions of such smooth muscles as the heart, glands and the digestive system
BORBORYGMUS	the medical term for rumbling stomach
BRAN	husks of cereal separated from flour during milling and often turned into fibrous foods
CARBOHYDRATES	a large group of organic compounds like sugar, starch, cellulose containing carbon, hydrogen and oxygen; a very important source of energy
CHOLERIC	bad tempered and bilious
COLONOSCOPY	an internal examination of the colon

CROHN'S DISEASE	the inflammation and thickening or ulceration of parts of the intestine
DIAPHRAGM	a tough, flat muscular layer which separates the chest cavity from the abdomen
DIVERTICULAR DISEASE	the formation of sacs and pouches on the outside of the intestine
DYSPEPSIA	medical term for upset stomach or indigestion
ENTERIC	anything to do with the intestines
ENZYMES	a group of proteins produced by the body's living cells to act as catalysts (speeding up agents) to chemical changes and reactions
FLORA	short for intestinal flora or the types of bacteria found in the gut
GALL-BLADDER	a sac attached to the duodenum; the store for bile, which is injected into the duodenum to aid the breakdown of food
GASTRO ENTEROLOGIST	a physician specialising in the digestive tract and its appendages
HALITOSIS	the clinical name for bad breath
HORMONE	substance produced by an endocrine gland and transported by the blood to the body areas where it can perform its own specific function
HYDROGEN BREATH TEST	a measure of the time taken for food to reach the large intestine
HYPERVENTILATION	breathing too deeply, or conversely breathing shallow and often
LACTASE	the enzyme which breaks down lactose or sugar into a more usable form
LACTOSE	the type of sugar found in milk

MUCUS	a secretion which acts as a lubricant and binding agent
PEPTIC	relating to the action of the digestive juices
PEPTIC ULCER	an ulceration of the mucous membrane lining that part of the digestive tract which is in contact with digestive juices
PERISTALSIS	the waves of muscular contraction which squeeze the food along the digestive passages
PLACEBO	a harmless substance prescribed to a patient who believes it to be a beneficial medicine
PROTEIN	a very large group of nitrogen based substances essential to proper body growth and function
PTYALIN	the enzyme found in saliva
RECEPTOR	the sensory nerve ending which changes electrical stimuli into muscular functions
SIGMOIDOSCOPE	a device used to examine the internal parts of the large intestine
SPASTIC COLON	the old name for some aspects of irritable bowel syndrome
SPHINCTER	a one-way valve sealing off a chamber
SYMPTOM	a sign that something is changing, or not well in the body
SYNDROME	a group of interacting symptoms
ULCERATIVE COLITIS	a disease of the colon
VILLI (singular villus)	the tiny spikes on the inside of the digestive tract. They increase the area in contact with foodstuffs and act as valves to let chosen products pass into the bloodstream

Useful Addresses

British Homoeopathic Association (Post Graduate Practitioners)
27A Devonshire Street, London W1N 1RJ
Tel: 071-935 2163

Society of Homoeopathy (Lay Professional Practitioners)
2 Artizan Road, Northampton NN1 4HU
Tel: 0604-21400

General Council & Register of Osteopaths
56 London Street, Reading, Berkshire RG1 4SQ
Tel: 0734-576585

Institute for Complementary Medicine
Unit 15, Tavern Quay, London SE16 1QZ
Tel: 071-237 5165

British Acupuncture Association & Register
22 Hockley Road, Rayleigh, Essex SS6 8EB
Tel: 0268-742534

Council for Acupuncture
179 Gloucester Place, London NW1 6DX
Tel: 071-724 5756

British Society for Allergy & Environmental Medicine
with **British Society of Nutritional Medicine**
ACORN, Romsey Road, Cadnam, Southampton SO4 2NM
Tel: 0703-812124

British Hypnotherapy Association
1 Wythburn Place, London W1H 5WL
Tel: 071-723 4443

General Council & Register of Consultant Herbalists
40 Sea Way, Middleton-on-Sea, West Sussex PO22 7SA
Tel: 0243-586012

General Council & Register of Naturopaths
6 Netherhall Gardens, London NW3 5RR
Tel: 071-435 8728

British Chiropractic Association
29 Whitley Street, Reading, Berkshire RG2 0EG
Tel: 0734-757557

International Federation of Aromatherapists
Royal Masonic Hospital, Ravenscourt Park, London W6 0TN
Tel: 081-846 8066

Association of Reflexologists
27 Old Gloucester Street, London WC1N 3XX
Tel: 071-237 6523

NOTES